GIFTS

Robin Gill is William Leec
Theology at Newcastle University and priest
St Mary's Church, Coldstream. He is married to a GP and has two children, both at university. In 1991 he left Newcastle to become the first Michael Ramsey Professor of Modern Theology at Canterbury.

Other titles available as Fount Paperbacks

The Archbishop of Canterbury's Lent Books

The Burning Bush   (*John Drury*)
Prayer and the Pursuit of Happiness   (*Richard Harries*)
The Way of the Cross   (*Richard Hollaway*)
Friendship with God   (*David Hope*)
Be Still and Know   (*Michael Ramsey*)
A Season for the Spirit   (*Martin Smith*)
Seeking God   (*Esther de Waal*)

By George Carey

The Great God Robbery

ROBIN GILL

GIFTS OF LOVE

FOREWORD BY THE
ARCHBISHOP OF CANTERBURY

Fount
An Imprint of HarperCollins*Publishers*

First published in Great Britain
in 1991 by Fount Paperbacks

Fount Paperbacks is an imprint of
HarperCollinsReligious
Part of HarperCollinsPublishers
77–85 Fulham Palace Road, London W6 8JB

Printed and bound in Great Britain
by HarperCollins Manufacturing, Glasgow

A catalogue record for this book is
available from the British Library

Biblical extracts are taken from the Revised English Bible (REV), a revision of
the New English Bible, © Oxford University Press and Cambridge University
Press 1989, and are used by kind permission of the copyright holders

CONTENTS

Acknowledgements

I am most grateful to quite a number of people for helping me with this book. It was prompted in the first place by Archbishop Robert Runcie, but then encouraged very warmly by Archbishop George Carey. They both could not have been kinder. My congregation have also been magnificent. First they had to listen to me preaching on gifts and testing out my ideas. Then they acted as guinea pigs one Lent on an outline of the material for this book. And finally individuals from the congregation and some of my academic colleagues read the later drafts of the book. I would particularly like to thank Jenny Gill, Joan Fox, John Sawyer, William Telford, Ian McDonald, Graham James and Paul Avis.

Foreword

Life is full of gifts. This book illustrates just how much all of us rely upon this bounty. Simply because we are given so much, we can neglect the Giver and perhaps not even see his offerings as gifts at all. For weakness and ignorance are no barrier to receiving, and enjoying, the gifts which come our way.

Lent is a time when many Christians stop a while to look more closely at the activity of God in every-day life. There will be much here to help them. Robin Gill explores his theme with imagination and sensitivity, reminding us of the miraculous gift which is our birth or how the gift of love comes so unexpectedly and undeservedly. God's own gift of love, embodied in Jesus Christ, is powerfully shown as the greatest of all good gifts. We are led from our experience of the world around us to the experience of Christ's passion and death at Calvary. That is why this makes such suitable Lenten reading.

I am very grateful to Robin Gill for writing this book. I am sure it will be a stimulus to faith and Christian growth for many people who will find that in studying it yet more gifts are brought their way.

+ George Cantuar

Introduction

I am an inveterate reader of books before going to sleep. More accurately, I have the same book by my bedside for a month or two. After three or four pages the eyes droop, the words become jumbles and I finally put the light out. Defeated again.

For other readers who suffer from this problem, I have written *Gifts of Love* in short sections. Just enough until sleep becomes too persistent. There is a section for every day, except Sunday, during the six weeks of Lent.

Of course you could read this book in more ambitious chunks. And there is no reason why it should be confined to Lent. It is intended to be flexible.

It is also intended for those struggling with faith as well as for those more comfortable with faith. But more of that in a moment.

Week 1

GIFTS IN A
SECULAR WORLD

1

The Gift of Birth

Few parents can ever forget the feelings they had when their first child was born. There seems to be no adequate preparation for these feelings. For many people they are quite unexpected. It is obviously possible to learn about the mechanics of childbirth. The ante-natal classes (ugh!), the videos, the booklets. All give information galore, but they scarcely convey feelings.

After our children are born, many of us love to retell the stories surrounding our various experiences. The newspapers bought but unread; the frenetic rush to hospital; the early – or was it the late? – arrival; the awkwardness of well developed pregnancy; the details of the birth . . . in full Technicolor, of course; all those jobs around the house not quite completed; the fraught arguments about suitable names; and the even fraughter arguments about suitable names for the grandparents . . . and many other things besides.

In our case it even included a moment of great irony. After my initial panic caused by the first contractions, I was persuaded to drive my wife calmly to the hospital. For a while all went well. But half-way there a policeman signalled us to stop. Something wrong with the car? Reckless driving? An accident in front, blocking the road for the next ten hours . . . followed naturally by a dramatic helicopter airlift?

No, it was just a traffic census. Today of all days. We smiled to each other as he solemnly asked us to pull over.

Immediately a smart young man – probably a student recruited for the task – leant into the car. "What is the reason for your journey?" he asked us confidently. Together we triumphantly chorused, "Well actually . . ."

His confidence disappeared at once. So did my panic. He turned white as I turned pink. Instead of filling in his questionnaire, we had to persuade him not to order a police escort to the hospital. And, yes, we were all right . . . but we probably ought to leave now. Eventually we did leave, but still a little worried about whether or not *he* would cope. I would love to know how he eventually filled in his census form!

Yet none of this is about feelings. It is about the sur-rounding events. At the level of feelings most new parents feel extremely fragile. Here is a new life which is going to be wholly dependent upon us for many years to come. We did so little to create that life ourselves. Men even less than women. And yet here it is as a gift. We even talk about "giving birth".

It is not a neutral gift. As we will be seeing later, gifts are seldom neutral. For many the baby will be a planned and wanted gift. Even unplanned, it may still be wanted. Yet sadly, for others a baby will be a thoroughly unwanted gift. Gifts frequently evoke strong feelings, for some *a* baby will be wanted, but not the particular baby that is born. Perhaps it is a boy not a girl, or a girl not a boy. Or perhaps the baby is handicapped. So, to add to the usual fears and feelings of fragility of new parents, there are added anguishes about handicap and deformity.

Yet having said that, many of those who express most strongly a feeling that their baby is a gift are those who have struggled the most or those who have learned to love their handicapped baby. Down's syndrome babies are frequently described by their parents as particular gifts of love. And those who have struggled for years to become pregnant will need to be told nothing about their babies being gifts.

The term GIFT has even been used to denote one of the new techniques for helping infertile couples. Amidst the bewildering array of new techniques offered by modern biotechnology, there is one with a more human-sounding name than most. The transfer of gametes within the womb – or gamete intra-fallopian transfer – has adopted the appropriate acronym GIFT. For once a medical label – not usually renowned for sensitivity – expresses very well the feelings of the couples involved. However intrusive the biotechnological methods might seem to outsiders, for the couples themselves the resulting babies, perhaps after years of infertility, truly appear as gifts.

Birth highlights something that is a part of our everyday life. At moments of heightened experience – as we shall be seeing in several contexts – we seem to become aware that life is a gift. We repeatedly use the language of gifts. Our imagery surrounding birth is imagery based upon the notion of gifts. At our most fragile and vulnerable we feel ourselves to be the recipients of gifts.

Of course the intensity of these feelings fades, but the feelings themselves are never wholly lost. Our language of "giving birth" still carries the traces. And however sizeable our children eventually become, those earliest memories remain.

Somewhat impatiently we listen to the birth stories of other families. Like home-videos they may not be for public consumption. "I am sure you would love to see our

17

family video." I am sure you would not! Yet naturally our own stories are enduringly fascinating. In families they get told and retold – even when all are thoroughly familiar with their every detail.

The heightened experiences surrounding birth offer a clue. The notion and language of gifts occurs spontaneously and naturally in secular experience. And birth as a gift is a notion that recurs again and again in religious imagery. But that is a clue for later.

MEDITATION

Isaiah 9:2-6

2

The Theme

I have long been fascinated by the way we talk about babies as "gifts", about people being "gifted", and about things as "given" in the world around us. We do this even in quite secular contexts, and we do it when religious issues are apparently far from our minds. In fact we do this so often in everyday speech that we seldom notice the religious origins of this language.

This Lent I am going to look at gifts. Starting with everyday uses of the term, I will only slowly unpack some of their religious meanings. I have deliberately written this book for those on the edge of faith and for those who wish to stand with them.

I can imagine that those who feel more comfortable with the Christian faith will be a little surprised by this decision. Lent books are supposed to be for those who already consider themselves to be Christians, yet who wish to deepen their faith. Such books are a way for congregations to learn together during Lent. Some Bible study, some ways to pray, some exploration of theology . . . surely these are the themes expected in Lent books.

Be patient. Especially if you already feel comfortable in your faith. By starting with secular experience, I believe that all of us can learn to look at faith afresh. If religious faith really is a live option today, then it must connect with, and make sense of, everyday experience. And if religiously committed people are to learn how to share their faith with others, then I believe that we will have to start from experiences which are apparently quite secular.

By looking for clues to faith in everyday experience we can become religious explorers together. The divisions between "believers" and "unbelievers" can be temporarily put to one side. Doubtless these are real divisions which may be important in other contexts. However, for the moment I would prefer to suspend them. "Gifts" in everyday life – deep and sometimes disturbing gifts – are a part of common experience, experience shared by believers and unbelievers alike. They are not the property of any single group.

Nevertheless this *is* a Lent book. Its object is slowly to build up a vision of faith from clues to be found in everyday experience. Gradually I will try to persuade the reader that religious understandings of "gifts" do make sense.

And, what is more important, that they do make sense of everyday experience.

There can be no compulsion here. There are no knock-down arguments which will force sceptics to believe against their better judgement. Faith would hardly be faith if this were possible. Everyday experience can always be treated simply and solely as mundane, humdrum experience. Ventures of faith can always be resisted.

The celebrated sociologist Max Weber described himself in later life as being "religiously unmusical". He spent a lifetime analysing religion in ways that still prove immensely illuminating. He made connnections about the different ways religion and society function which remain stimulating and intellectually exciting. Yet, after all this, he found that he could never return to the faith of his youth. In this sense, then, he finally felt himself to be "religiously unmusical".

His image remains a powerful one. It is possible to analyse the sounds that make up music for others, but never to hear them as music for oneself. And it is possible to view what other people consider to be great works of art, simply as interesting paint sticking to a canvas. Similarly, it is possible to look at the clues which lead others to faith, yet never to share that faith oneself. There can be no compulsion to make the religious connections which will be suggested here.

Forget about compulsion. Faith is about seeing and about vision. It resonates most powerfully in stories, symbols, rituals and parables. And it has much in common with art and with music. All can be means to new understandings . . . understandings which go far beyond words. And in each, new connections can be made tentatively and in a spirit of exploration.

This is how I would like you to use this book. Lent is a good time to make religious explorations. A time to look afresh and to make new connections.

MEDITATION

Ephesians 1

3

Being Gifted

We talk about people being "gifted". The term is used so frequently that its peculiarity in a secular world tends to elude us. A person who is "gifted" is a person with special "skills" or "abilities". "Gifted" people are people with exceptional "talents". But there is more to the term than that.

The fact that we mix these various terms together tends to blind us to the oddity of the term "gifted" itself. "Skills" and "abilities" seem to refer to inherent properties within individuals. Like a good head of hair, sparkling teeth, or blue eyes, they are accidents of birth.

The term "talents" has roots in the Bible and earlier in Greek culture – suggesting the notion of people being endowed with different "talents" which they can use or not. In the Greek world a "talent" of gold was as much gold as a man could carry. In the New Testament parable, three individuals are given differing "talents" of gold, which two use to good effect but one buries unused. From these roots the term today refers to special qualities which individuals possess (but which they can still waste), rather than to vast accumulations of wealth.

However, the term "gifts" suggests something far stranger. We talk about artists as being "gifted", as well as mathematicians, scientists, chess players, musicians and even athletes. What we notice in all of these areas is that some people seem to excel in ways which the rest of us can admire but never emulate. Even though we may ourselves play music, paint pictures, play chess or take part in sports, we know that compared with them we will never be anything other than enthusiastic amateurs.

So a part of me would have loved to have been a great trumpeter. Yet in reality I know that, even after playing the instrument for thirty years, I don't actually have sufficient musical gifts. The young American trumpeter Winton Marsalis or the Swedish virtuoso Hakan Hardenberger, on the other hand, do have such gifts.

Winton Marsalis seems to be equally as "gifted" at playing jazz as he is at playing classical music. His interpretation of Haydn's over-familiar (for a trumpeter at least) concerto is startlingly original. Having murdered this trumpet concerto for years, I can now listen to it again with pleasure. And Hakan Hardenberger is so technically "gifted" that several modern composers have written music for him which few other trumpeters can play, let alone perform in public.

And, to make matters worse, neither of *them* has been

playing the instrument for thirty years. Now of course they both practise more assiduously than I do. But, at the risk of being too personal, that is not the most obvious difference between us as trumpeters. I am aware that, even if I abandoned theology and practised the trumpet feverishly day and night, I could never approach their level of playing. Quite simply, I lack their "gifts".

What does this mean? Does it mean that some people are accidentally born with lips shaped suitably for trumpet playing? Obviously that matters . . . up to a point. Yet it is really not very obvious that great trumpet players all have the same shaped lips. Anyone who remembers the curious indentations on Louis Armstrong's lips will realize that. Or is it good breath control? Again that is obviously important. However, every trumpeter is taught never to puff one's cheeks out whilst playing. It is bad technique. Yet the great Dizzy Gillespie has been doing just that for decades.

And religious imagery abounds in descriptions of musicians who excel. It is the terms "talents" and "gifts" that recur repeatedly, not just "skills" and "abilities".

So, in a review of the autobiography of that extraordinary young percussionist, Evelyn Glennie, one newspaper noted:

At about the same time as this talented musician went deaf from causes unknown, she discovered a passion for percussion. She compensated for her hearing-loss by developing an extraordinary awareness of vibration . . . In fact, deafness appears to have spurred on her fierce determination to succeed. She says she suffered no disappointment on learning that her condition was inoperable: Because I had to concentrate with every fibre of my body, I experienced music with a profundity that I felt was God-given and precious.

The truly "gifted" musicians seem to bring something else, quite beyond technique, to music. Like "gifted" people in many other fields they often seem to defy conventional wisdom and accepted practices. The truly "gifted" appear to the rest of us to be somewhat uncontrollable. They elicit our respect but also some fear. They stimulate, but they also disrupt the conventional.

Gifts can both excite and frighten.

MEDITATION

Ephesians 4:1-13

4

The Gifted Musician

Perhaps of all musicians, the one that is most widely regarded as especially gifted is Mozart. Peter Shaffer's controversial play *Amadeus* picks up this point beautifully.

The play struggles with the paradox of how awesome music could have emerged from such a vulgar and flippant young man. It contrasts Mozart with the older and seemingly upright composer Salieri, who was literally driven mad with jealousy. Salieri was the respected composer in court circles. Yet he knew in private that the brat Mozart was a musical genius in a way that he, Salieri, could never be. It was Mozart who was "loved by God" (the literal meaning of Mozart's middle name, Amadeus). And it was Mozart's musical talents which were quite simply "gifts". Seemingly music was channelled through him from God.

The play and the film that was based upon it are full of sharp contrasts. There is the other-worldly beauty of Mozart's music clashing with the this-worldly behaviour of Mozart himself. There is the pathetic figure of Salieri ranting in squalid madness at the end, looking back to the youthful, but now dead, Mozart. There are the hours Mozart spent at infantile parties contrasting with times of frenetic composing. There is the death-like figure commissioning the haunting, but finally unfinished, Requiem. In every scene the strangeness of Mozart's prodigious gifts is apparent.

Amadeus, although much admired as a play, has also been the subject of considerable controversy. It seems to suggest that Salieri actually murdered Mozart as a result of his jealousy. In several other respects the playwright goes well beyond the historical evidence. Be that as it may, the point that the play makes is a serious one and indeed a deeply religious one. There *is* something mysterious about prodigious musical achievements; and those who attain them have themselves frequently used religious terms to describe the process by which they are "created" (itself a religious term). Mozart was no exception.

Clear evidence for this is to be found in some of the surviving letters from Mozart and his father. Leopold Mozart did indeed believe that his son's precocious talents were "gifts". In one of the earliest letters, written when Wolfgang was just seven years old, his father wrote:

> The latest is that, upon going to the organ for our diversion, I explained the use of the pedal to Wolferl. He immediately began to try it, thrust the stool aside, and preluded, standing and treading the pedals, and that, indeed, as if he had practised for many months previously. Everyone was astonished and (indeed it) is a new grace of God, such as many receive only after much effort.

A few months later the proud father wrote again as follows:

> Four sonatas by Mr Wolfgang Mozart are being engraved! Do but picture to yourself the stir these sonatas will make in the world when it is set forth on the title-page that this is the work of a child of seven years; and, when the incredulous are challenged to put the matter to the proof (as has happened already), he invites someone to write down a minuet, or suchlike, and then forthwith (without touching the clavier) sets down the bass and, if desired, the second violin part besides! In due course you will hear how good these sonatas are . . . I can assure you that God daily works new miracles in this child.

Written about almost anyone else this would soon be dismissed as the vain boasts of an over-ambitious father. Yet, however ambitious Leopold undoubtedly was, even the earliest music of his son is still played and admired today. The "gifts" that he had simply defied explanation.

He was able to do things musically, sometimes without practice, quite beyond the reach of most other people.

Further, and stranger still, Mozart himself clearly had only limited insight into the creative impulses that surged through him. Writing as an adult, he depicted them as follows:

> When I am, as it were, completely myself, entirely alone, and of good cheer – say, travelling in a carriage, or walking after a good meal, or during the night when I cannot sleep; it is on such occasions that my ideas flow best and most abundantly. *Whence* and *how* they come, I know not; nor can I force them. Those ideas that please me I retain in memory, and am accustomed, as I have been told, to hum them to myself. If I continue in this way, it soon occurs to me how I may turn this or that morsel to account, so as to make a good dish of it, that is to say, agreeably to the rules of counterpoint, to the peculiarities of the various instruments, etc.
>
> All this fires my soul, and, provided I am not disturbed, my subject enlarges itself, becomes methodized and defined, and the whole, though it be long, stands almost complete and finished in my mind, so that I can survey it, like a fine picture or a beautiful statue, at a glance . . . What has been thus produced I do not easily forget, and this is perhaps the best gift I have my Divine Maker to thank for.

Only at this point did he write anything down!

This letter gives a remarkable glimpse – just a glimpse, no more – into creative genius. The Catholic Mozart, although highly flippant in many of his letters, uses the language of "gifts". He appears as puzzled as anyone else about the source of his musical ideas; and he seems to prepare himself only for their reception, selection and presentation. He thus perceives them in terms almost external to himself.

MEDITATION

1 Kings 3:4-15

5

The Gifted Sportsman

But perhaps all of this is too rarefied and dated. Do people really resort to the once religious language of "talents" and "gifts" when trying to describe individuals today who excel at something? In most fields the mundane language of "skills" and "abilities" might now appear more natural.

For an experiment I turned to the sports pages of the newspaper that I have just read. What terms are used here to depict individuals who excel at sport?

Kriss Akabusi has just won the gold medal in the 400 metres hurdles at Split. The headline, in traditional punning style, reads "Akabusi, the On-song Christian Soldier". It makes a special feature of the fact that Akabusi is known to be a Christian and conducts daily prayer meetings for fellow believers in the British team.

The story opens as follows:

The notion that athletes can be too nice for their own good was laid to rest this week when Kriss Akabusi, soldier and devout Christian, became a substantial champion, much to the delight of everyone who believes in the brotherhood of man.

It suggests that Akabusi usually responds quietly to winning races. His typical response is "simply offering up thanks for the energy and rhythm" that enables him to win. However, on this famous occasion he was quite different:

> Guaranteeing that he will figure prominently in every television montage compiled at the end of another sporting year, Akabusi responded with glee, running every which way until falling to his knees in prayer.
>
> He is not normally given to such behaviour and it was entirely spontaneous. "I went loopy", he confessed. Nobody took offence or backed off in embarrassment because it is generally agreed that Akabusi deserves everything good that comes his way.

And then his coach adds:

> A lot of athletes cross the line, glance at their time and they are already thinking about a lap of honour. Kriss simply gave himself up to the moment and of course the bonus of the record set him alight.

Gifts are not mentioned directly in this story. Yet they are clearly implicit within it. Akabusi is depicted as typically "offering up thanks", but on this occasion as "falling to his knees in prayer". The religious, and indeed moral, underlay is quite explicit.

Perhaps this also is too easy. Akabusi, as a member of the Salvation Army, is more overtly religious than most people in sport. Clues in a less religious context might be more convincing.

On the opposite page of the newspaper there is one of those recurrent stories about the bad behaviour on court of the tennis player John McEnroe. The headline here – this time a splendidly mixed metaphor – is "McEnroe Facing Grand Slam Guillotine". The gist of the story is that McEnroe has already been fined $7000 during the current tennis season for bad behaviour and is likely soon to exceed the limit of $7500.

One minor tantrum (by his standards) would be enough for John McEnroe to be banned from the Australian Open in January, curtailing the American's plan to return to the scene of his disqualification. An abusive squawk or an imprudent swing of the racket here at the United States Open would be sufficient to incur the $500 fine that stands between McEnroe and suspension from the next Grand Slam tournament.

At 31, McEnroe no longer has time to waste, and yet his lack of self-control continues to handicap what remains of a wonderful talent.

Now here are both of the features noticed earlier. The term "talent", with its religious roots, is used in preference to more mundane terms. And there is also the strong hint that it is a talent which is exceedingly difficult to control.

The article continues with details of his recent matches and the difficulties that he will face next. It concludes:

It is likely to prove hard work for McEnroe, and many

experienced observers are shaking their heads and lamenting that the player's gifts have rarely been strengthened by the perspiration of totally dedicated preparation.

So, once again, it is the language of "gifts" that is used – albeit this time to depict the qualities characteristic of a tennis player who excels, yet who remains deviant.

MEDITATION

Galatians 6:3-10

6

The Given

Again, even in an apparently secular age, we still talk about things in the world around us as being "given". Indeed, science is founded on the belief that the world really will respond to our rational enquiries. So great discoveries about the physical world can still be made by mathematicians engaged in pure thought. Einstein's discoveries about relativity were worked out on paper before they were tested through physical experiments.

We live, it seems, in a world in which there really is a correspondence between pure thought and the way that physical reality works. And scientists, themselves committed to the idea of rational "discovery", still tend to talk about things being "given" ("given" is the literal meaning of "data").

This is not of course to claim that all scientists see the world in religious terms. Some do, some don't. As it happens physical scientists tend to be more conventionally religious than social scientists or philosophers. However that is not my point. It is simply this: scientists, like those involved in the creative arts, still use terms with deep religious roots. They tend to talk about "creativity" and "inspiration". They personalize "nature". They have "vocations". They undergo a lengthy "schooling". They form a "profession". They are regarded as "dedicated". And they talk about "the given".

Some of these terms derive from the monastic world. It is monks and nuns who have "vocations" (callings), who are "schooled" and then "professed". Others derive from more general religious vocabulary. Yet all have clear religious roots.

Now, of course, all of this can be easily dismissed. It can be argued that the origins of terms need not trouble present-day users of those terms. Just because we use terms like "gifts" in ways which have obvious religious roots, that does not mean that we must remain committed to those roots.

So, we do talk about some jobs as "vocations", regardless of whether the individuals involved do or do not feel themselves to have been "called" by God to do them. In fact, the list of jobs that are popularly depicted as "vocations" is itself rather variable. Some jobs — especially those of doctors and clergy — nearly always qualify, whereas others might or might not. In any case, religious terms become secular and apparently no longer need religious support.

This is a valid argument. Yet the point I will try to develop in the course of Lent is that *if* you take the religious context of "gifts" seriously, then you will gain a deeper understanding even of the everyday world.

Strictly speaking, no one *needs* to make the connections I will be seeking to make. Quite obviously they can be resisted – although even this has dangers. Terms carry meanings, and inherited terms carry meanings that may resurface unexpectedly in the future. Religious roots may be ignored for the present. But, if they genuinely point to experiences that are part of the human condition, they may not be ignored for ever. Then, as happened so forcibly in modern Iran, they may flood through the dams of current scepticism. Better, perhaps, to reflect on religious roots in tranquillity now, than to risk the damaging floods of some future fundamentalism.

Yet still there can be no compulsion here. Creative religious thinking should always be a matter of exploration and choice. However, if you choose to follow this particular path, there are I believe some discoveries to be made.

MEDITATION

Matthew 20:20-28

Week 2

GIFTS OF LOVE

7

An Unexpected Gift

All summer we watched a pair of moorhens taking over our new pond. It was all quite unexpected. The hours of careful planning – round or square or oblong; larger or smaller; deeper or shallower? The incredibly healthy digging on cold Northumbrian days in the middle of winter – frost and ice permitting. And then the expensive visits to the local garden centre: a dozen goldfish and three exotic water lilies.

None of this had moorhens in mind. Certainly the goldfish did not. Their predecessors had survived for four years in the old pond, growing large and plump despite some severe winters.

Then one spring morning there was a statuesque heron standing nearby, looking well breakfasted. The new goldfish surfaced just once and then vanished. And the water lilies are exotic no more. They still send out an occasional leaf. But they are invariably pecked, battered and finally snapped.

If I had been designing a moorhen pond it would have been quite different. There would have been an island safely surrounded by water, with lush cover around the edges for comfort and protection, and hardy marsh marigolds, not fragile water lilies. And definitely no goldfish at 70p a gobble.

The moorhens knew nothing of this. Presumably what they saw was some tempting water and plenty of overgrown bushes in which to hide (it *is* a country garden).

They might even have spotted my goldfish. Whatever, they quickly established squatter's rights.

Then there were six moorhens – or rather two moorhens and four moorchicks. Four untidy circles of dark brown feathers following two elegant parents. If people emerged from the house they immediately rushed for those overgrown bushes. However, from the kitchen window we could watch them undisturbed. The curious cooting sound of the adults responding to the anxious cheeps of the chicks. The dipping movement of the adults as they browsed in the grass – like somewhat eccentric mannequins, placing each outsized foot directly in front of the next – and the clumsy hops of youngsters constantly demanding to be fed.

Yet this is nature, not Disneyland. Soon one of the four drowned and another was killed by a weasel. When the mother saw the weasel she attacked it fearlessly. This timid, cautious bird suddenly became a ferocious flurry of wings, shrieks and beak. But it was too late. Doubtless the weasel had hungry youngsters too. And this was a chance for a succulent meal.

Once a chick was dead, the adult moorhens concentrated only on the living. Even when a chick floated in the middle of the pond, pathetically drowned, they ignored it.

When a third chick disappeared, the father left too. Up to that point the adults had shared their parental duties admirably – no expectation here that the woman would do all the cooking, washing up and changing of nappies. Indeed, until we learned to distinguish between them by the length of the orange crest above their beak, we could detect no obvious difference from their responses to the young. Both fed them, protected them, taught them to swim, and answered their incessant calls. With a single chick left, this changed. Now it was just mother and child. How typical!

Slowly the chick has matured into an adult. It has developed the same sleek lines as the mother, the same cooting sound and the same dipping movement. The wings, now tipped with white, have become airworthy and the plumage begins to sheen. It is still too early for me to be sure whether this is a male or a female – a moorhen or a moorcock, so to speak. The orange crest is yet to develop. Mother and child still browse together in the grass and take it in turns to swim in the pond.

To depict all of this as love is perhaps too human centred. The bonds between the two adults, between the adults and the chicks, and finally between the mother and child, are strong but temporary. They are the bonds of propagation rather than sentiment. Their object is to ensure that moorhens survive . . . even at the expense of my goldfish and lilies!

Yet for us as humans they have certainly acted as unexpected gifts of love – the excitement of seeing the chicks for the first time; the drama of the weasel; the pathos of the drowning; the gradual maturing of the surviving chick; and especially the bond between mother and child and their enduring elegance. All these annual routines of the natural world – normally hidden from us – have for once been acted out in full view of our kitchen window.

MEDITATION

Psalm 148

8

The Gift of Peace

Gifts are seldom neutral. Because they are typically unearned and are frequently unusual or unexpected, they catch our attention and quickly elicit value-judgements. Gifts excite. The prospect of Christmas gifts can over-excite small children for weeks beforehand, as many exasperated parents will know only too well. Gifts are also the characteristic way to show affection. Gifted people fascinate us. And gifts from other people engage us.

Even gifts of poison achieve most of the these things. However, that is a theme for next week. For the moment, it is gifts of love which need unravelling. Gifts of love do not simply engage us – they enrich our lives.

Slowly we are beginning to realize this. If once it was thought to be sentimental and outdated to be a lover of the countryside, today it is again becoming fashionable. Less than a generation ago it was the city which was considered to be the centre of civilization and culture. The natural world was there to serve the growing needs of city dwellers. More fossil fuels to serve their rapidly increasing demands for energy and transport. More timber to meet their voracious need for paper. More food to sustain a world population that was doubling every few years. More airports, more motorways, more oil terminals, more reservoirs, more new towns, more ribbon development . . . each reducing the countryside with every new decade.

Gradually a different vision is emerging. Endless urban growth and the associated destruction of the countryside are no longer so acceptable. Green issues are less often dismissed as mere romanticism. It does matter what we do to our environment. It does matter that we are hunting whales to extinction. It does matter that we are destroying wildlife through our industrial pollution. And it does matter that deforestation and intensive farming may be altering our very atmosphere.

A One World vision suggests something far more positive. The world around us is a unique gift of love. It is full of surprises and delights, which can enrich our lives, and which we destroy quite literally at our peril. This world is to be enjoyed through conservation, not through exploitation. As humans we are heirs to a gift, not lords of the universe. Gratitude, not arrogance, should be our response.

Again, the prospect of nuclear destruction has provoked a new vision. Maintaining a balance of nuclear terror was once thought to be the most effective way to keep peace between East and West. Mutual Assured Destruction was for long official policy shared by NATO and the Warsaw Pact. It was argued that it would prevent any possible use in the world of nuclear weapons. Whilst the world was so polarized, the policy might have appeared to be plausible. In a fluid and more volatile world it makes little sense.

Nuclear proliferation has ensured that these appalling weapons of destruction are no longer the exclusive property of two mutually deterred blocks of nations. Israel has nuclear weapons, so does South Africa, China and India. Parts of the Arab world are desperately seeking them, as well as parts of South America. Soon they will be everywhere. Someone, somewhere, will surely use them. A tyrant who has nothing to lose? A sophisticated terrorist group? Whatever it may be. We have created a monster fast running out of control. Past warnings have gone unheeded.

The new vision suggests that, if we are to survive as a species, then we cannot rely indefinitely on peace being kept by threats of mass destruction. To remain credible such threats must be continually increased through ever more powerful weapons of destruction. Yet these very weapons, given their inevitable spread through the international arms trade, actually make the world increasingly dangerous. In contrast to a peace based on a threat of war, true peace is a gift of love.

Peace as a gift of love in the world is a vision not a reality. Nations are still painfully locked into peace based upon threats. Yet if we are actually to survive, we may have to learn other ways and to trust other visions. Gifts of love might need to become a reality between nations.

MEDITATION
Luke 6:27-38

9

Animals as Gifts

For many individuals gifts of love are already a reality. In a destructive and potentially dangerous world, it is often in the narrow protection of our homes that we know about gifts of love. The contrast is a sharp one. The world at large is frequently judged to be unloving. Through our televisions, radios and newspapers we daily reinforce this judgement. Love is known privately not publicly. It is in our homes that gifts of love can become real.

Of course this is an exaggeration. Homes are not always places of love. And the world at large can sometimes show surprising outbursts of love. Yet the privacy of love runs deeply in our culture. It carries with it serious dangers of escapism. Yet it also offers clues . . . especially about gifts. Nowhere is this more obvious than in our responses to the animals that share our homes.

Every Christmas public warnings are made against giving animals to people as unexpected gifts. Every year animals are given as pets, are liked for a short while, and then disposed of. It is odd that an animal-loving nation is also a nation that requires vets to destroy pets once they have satisfied some short-lived fancy. It is also ironic that vets, who have trained for years to save animals and who usually became vets in the first place because of their profound love for animals, are required by us to do such things.

Our ambivalence to animals is even carried in our everyday language. Of someone who behaves appallingly we

43

say that "he behaved like an animal". We frequently use this simile when in reality non-human animals would typically behave in no such way. It is to depict human behaviour that we have had to invent terms such as "genocide" or "concentration camps". And it is humans, not other animals, that rack their brains to invent ever more ingenious ways of destroying their own kind.

Yet for most of us domestic animals are valued more highly than this. When an old and much loved dog finally dies, it is difficult not to feel pangs of emptiness. A "friend" is no longer there. A nuzzle, a touch, a stroke, is missing. Despite our theoretical distinctions between people and animals, we can grieve for both. In fact, for some people the depth of grief that they experience at the death of one animal can deter them from ever getting another. It is not that they have stopped being animal lovers. Rather the opposite. It is precisely because they remain such animal lovers that they can no longer face the intimate death of another.

In the long relationship between people and dogs, stretching back thousands of years and across many different cultures, there have been many shared lives. We personify dogs. We give them people's names. We talk to them and ascribe to them gifts of understanding well beyond their doggy brains. And on the whole we don't eat them. There have been occasional reports of dog-eating cultures or of dogs being discovered in the freezers of more dubious restaurants. But for most of us these are aberrations. We would almost as soon eat people!

For the lonely and the vulnerable the dog can be trusted in a way that people cannot be. The virtues that we ascribe to dogs are "devotion", "dependability" and "faithfulness". And evidence which suggests that dogs do not always have these virtues, is difficult for us to assimilate. The dog both protects and comforts. Because of their territorial nature, household dogs can be relied upon to guard our properties. We continue to hold this belief even when we laconically admit that our particular dog would "probably end up licking any burglar". Affection and protection combined.

The feel of living fur can be a source of great strength and comfort to the sick and to the infirm. Cats can be stroked and fondled. Touch, at once both important and so often denied to the infirm and to the lonely, can be provided instead by the pet. The cat or the dog makes no distinctions between people who are old, or infirm, or feel themselves to be unattractive to other people. They respond to warmth, food, shelter and touch. And in return they are treated as gifts of love.

Animals are not machines. Their behaviour is never wholly predictable. Even after a dozen years their idiosyncrasies can still amuse. I have often thought that the family dog has, in some respects, been given the role in our culture once occupied by the medieval clown. They are an intimate "part of the family", but disgracefully lack the manners of the family. They respond to laughter and to disapproval. They have tricks to perform and confidences to keep. They can be deviant. They breed only when we allow it or when our attention is distracted. Within certain bounds, they are allowed to destroy our homes. And, of course, they greatly amuse us.

On any understanding of "gifts" animals are important. They are a "given" part of our planet, which we human animals ignore at our peril. And in many of our homes they can indeed be "gifts of love".

MEDITATION

Psalm 150

10

Life as a Gift

At moments of heightened experience we can become especially aware that life is a gift. This is particularly so in the intimate presence of birth or death.

The feelings of fragility and vulnerability experienced by parents at the birth of their first child may well be experienced by them again at the loss of their own elderly parents. Even when the parents have been confused and cantankerous, and when everyone else is assuring them that their death is "a merciful release", it doesn't usually feel that way. Instead there is a void, a deep ache and longing.

Perhaps it is a longing for parental pride. "Look at me and at how well I am doing!" Achieving anything is so much more satisfying when behind the achievement there is the glow of the proud parent. Even the remnant of the parent will do. It is enough that they are still there, still able to underpin us as their children. With their death this is all gone.

Or perhaps it is the ache for things not said, for reconciliations not made, or just for stories never quite finished. "I will ask father." But I can't. The moment has passed and it can never return . . . at least not in this life. There can be no more words. No more memories shared or forgivenesses sought. It is all so final.

In desperation some people turn to mediums for solace . . . one final message. The medium is the message . . . or that is the hope at least. Trading on grief and vulnerability, the mediums appear to offer one last contact, one last word, one last reassurance that all is finally well.

Their solace depends so obviously upon carefully studied ambiguity. We *want* them to be genuine and, what is more, they know that we do. Sometimes their "spiritual" powers depend upon less than spiritual tricks. One medium placed short-wave radios in the audience in order to listen to shared confidences before the show began. Another computerized all letters received from members of the public, and then sent them free invitations to the show when it came to their area. The vulnerable became dupes. "The spirits tell me that there is someone here called George who has lost a small child." Poor grieving George is thrilled – temporarily.

For a while we might overlook their guesses and mistakes, their leading questions and their vacuous messages. We might deny that their "spiritual" powers have mundane and impure origins. But not for ever. Spiritual deceits seldom conquer deep aches and longings.

Or perhaps it is the void of realizing that we are now

the old. The generations have shifted. When we became parents most of us still had parents. Now we are parents without parents. Perhaps we are grandparents too. Our vulnerability becomes a cry of mortality. The gift of life is passing.

It is surely no accident that precisely at these moments many people start to take a new interest in roots and family trees. If you visit any County Record Office you will soon make this discovery. My academic research requires me to spend many hours beavering away in a variety of archives. And always it is the same story.

A middle-aged couple, armed with pencils and note-books, arrive. They approach the enquiry desk. "I am not sure whether we have come to the right place . . . but we have an unusual request. We would like to investigate our family tree." And always the staff respond in the same courteous way. They express first surprise and interest and then patiently explain about the mysteries of microfilms. Yet they also look so relieved when they discover that I have not come to investigate my ancestors . . . at least, not usually!

Through these aches and longings we can also glimpse that life is a gift. It is unpredictable and full of surprises. It is fleeting and elusive. Yet it is also precious and to be treasured. Time itself appears as a gift. It is to be enjoyed today, because tomorrow it may be gone. Gifts can be wasted. So can time. So can life. Or they can be received with joy and used whilst they are given to us.

It is perhaps for this reason that suicide is so corrosive. When a friend takes their own life it threatens our lives too. Frequently we find ourselves saying, "What a waste of gifts!" We console ourselves that their mind was temporarily unhinged. For surely it must have been? Faced with the gift of life, the most precious gift in the world, who would willingly choose to reject it? Yet some do, or at least appear so to do. And in the process they challenge the principle that runs throughout nature . . . survival.

Faced with the death of a young person, for whatever reason, it is the language of gifts that recurs again and again. "They had so much to give!" This surely is the reason for the enduring obsession with the "gifted" poet Sylvia Plath. Other poets have resonated language and shaped the culture of their times. Few of them have had their graves vandalized and their lives picked over minutely in a variety of biographies. By taking her own life so young, Sylvia Plath became not just a gifted poet but an icon. Her gifts have been turned into secular relics.

One of the hardest tasks for a priest is to take the funeral of a young person. I will never forget the grief of the family of a boy of eighteen killed in a stupid motorbike accident. We sat up all night together watching his broken body heaving rhythmically in response to the respirator. At dawn the doctor pronounced him dead. The heaving stopped and the tears began. And the church was packed. Somehow I knew that I must survive the service. If I broke down whilst reading the service, everyone else would break down. Their dignity depended upon my control. Few priests find this easy.

Yet from the ashes of their grief the parents themselves became a strength to others. For the next few years they could console other parents who had lost young children as no others could, precisely because they had shared their grief. Whereas others could only weep, they could offer vision and strength. It was they who could talk about gifts.

Their child had been a gift, a precious gift, whom they had loved and enjoyed. Beyond the pain and grief, their love and joy persisted. Life is a gift. Even short and fleeting life is a gift.

And, despite death, life remains a gift.

MEDITATION

Genesis 4:1-10

11

Gifts from Love

Parts of modern medicine have served to reinforce this vision. Fears of new technology have sometimes produced terrifying versions of the future. Aldous Huxley's nightmare of babies produced only in factories; the androids of space fiction; the Frankenstein monster; the half-human/half-animal clones of some future biotechnology.

The reality of biotechnology is somewhat different; babies born to otherwise infertile couples; hopes that genetic disorders may one day be corrected; viruses tailored to attack diseases rather than people; new grain seed developed to feed a hungry world. Whatever abuses must be guarded against, the benefits of biotechnology could bring life where otherwise there was only death. The gift of life.

Even the tragic death of young motor-cyclists can be partially transformed. When that respirator was switched off all those years ago, that was the end. The body was buried and the family was left to grieve. Today his organs might have been used to bring life to others. Through the appalling tragedy of young life wasted, there is a glimmer of hope for those that grieve. Their boy's life has been lost. But his kidneys, and perhaps even his heart, might bring new hope to someone else. At the bleakest moment of their grief, families can glimpse the prospects of a new life. Modern medicine has made possible some remarkable gifts of love.

Amongst the most remarkable must be the heroic giving of live donors – siblings or parents giving one of their kidneys or some of their bone marrow to a child. Donating bone marrow repeatedly and at great pain is heroic indeed. A costly gift of love. And kidney transplants from live donors also appear as remarkable gifts of love. Families prepared to risk danger, excruciating pain and even death, to give life to one of their members. Like the fearless rush of the moorhen, such risk is not calculated coolly. If a brother or sister or child can be given new life, then it is a risk that many of us would unhesitatingly take.

Like all gifts it can be distorted. The shameful bribing of peasants from the Third World to give their kidneys to the affluent West is just such a distortion, a potent combination of bribery and ignorance, masquerading as caring medicine. Gifts are not neutral. Yet that should not blind us to the genuine gifts of love shown by family donors. This is love well beyond the demands of duty.

And at the end of life, there are countless unrecorded examples of gifts of love beyond duty: daughters looking after elderly and infirm parents, against the demands of nature, caring for them instead of having children themselves. Wives or husbands looking after senile spouses, doing tasks that they might once have thought disgusting and demeaning, often changing roles despite long-established stereotypes. Husbands doing jobs that in their youth belonged properly only to women, wives becoming strong when once they were thought, and perhaps taught, to be weak.

Gifts of love abound in the most unlikely places. Behind the gruff exterior of some old person known only in passing, there may be daily gifts of love to a senile spouse. Sometimes I have watched old couples caring for each other to the end, and long after their children have been demanding that "something must be done". Resisting homes, and hospitals, and their guilt-filled children, they have coped and cared.

When love is private such stories are told so seldom. But the privacy of love in our culture does not destroy gifts of love. Rather the gifts get locked behind household doors, they become anonymous and invisible. Yet the truth is that gifts of love are still to be found freely. However secular society might appear today, they still abound.

MEDITATION

Luke 10:25-37

12

The Gift of Self

But most of this could be seen merely as self-centred. Pets are "my" gifts. Even the very term "pets" denotes this for those who prefer the term "animal companions". Children are "my" gifts. People sometimes have children for the most selfish of reasons. For some unemployed girls, having a baby can become a means to benefits, housing and status which might otherwise be denied them. Elderly couples may care for each other for reasons which are as much selfish as selfless. Without their spouse they would simply be lonely and perhaps alone.

Even mourning is not selfless. We grieve for others even when we know that they were tired of living. And we grieve even when death has spared them further suffering or humiliation. All too often we mourn for ourselves and for our own loss, rather than for the loss of the gifts of the person or of the animal we love. A part of coming to terms with grief is indeed the realization of its lurking selfishness.

Pathological grief is just that. It is a pathology. It no longer has much to do with those who have died. Instead it has much to do with those who are still living. Like Queen Victoria mourning her long-dead Albert, grief can become a way of manipulating others. The pathological mourner requires privileges from others. Mourning has become a social role – a means of exacting social space.

Gifts of love excite "me". They redound to "my" credit. And it is "my" attention that is caught by them. Even the most selfless act can create self-satisfaction. Our self-centredness is boundless.

Yet some gifts can almost be selfless. One missionary still haunts me. I met him twenty years ago in Papua New Guinea. In my twelve months of theological college teaching in this remote island, he was one of the very few Westerners I met who had almost become local. He had identified almost completely with the Papua New Guinea people. Most of us, despite living in conditions that would horrify many in the West, had a clutter of possessions that were the envy of the local people.

We brought books and cameras, radios and recorders. We travelled on planes and ate Western food when local food became too dull for us. We lived amongst other Westerners and we seldom talked anything but English. We slept on beds and had our meals around tables.

Of course, by our Western standards there were considerable discomforts. There were endless mosquitoes exquisitely packed with malaria. Few of us avoided occasional bouts. We had ancient mosquito nets, but no fly-wire and certainly no air-conditioning. There were flies galore and enormous cockroaches, which particularly enjoyed hiding in the communal fridges. There was a whole squelch of toads – reputedly introduced by the Americans during the War to control the insect population. Whether true or not, they now thrived alongside the insects, crawling behind cupboards and bookshelves in every house. Once there, they stank.

Yet we were still Westerners in style and habit and outlook. Then briefly, very briefly, I met a priest who had almost ceased to be a Westerner. The things that we still clung to, he had abandoned. He lived as a local and worked tirelessly to foster local churches and local church leaders. Moving around on foot from place to place, he worked and he worked, giving self to others in a way that few others find possible.

I cannot say that I found him particularly easy. Mostly he ignored other Westerners, even on his brief visits to the centre for medical treatment. Perhaps he realized that this was the only way he could avoid resuming our Western styles and habits. Perhaps he was aware that we suspected that he was too paternalistic to the Papua New Guinea people themselves (an old missionary failing). Or perhaps he was simply shy of us as newcomers. I have no idea and I could never find out.

However, I was deeply impressed with his selfless giving. Here was an unsung Mother Teresa of the Anglican Church. A priest – possibly quite a simple priest – trying to live a Christ-like life as wholeheartedly as he was able.

Even then, there was one thing that he could not give up. He could give up Western comforts and company. He could give up having a wife and family. He could give up any prospects of an ecclesiastical career (one of the most insidious temptations for a priest). In truth, he could give self in ways beyond the wildest dreams of those of us with families, possessions and responsibilities. Yet there was one thing that even he could never give up . . . the chance to get out.

When he became terminally ill, he was flown out to a hospital in Australia. To be a Papua New Guinean properly there can be no escape. You are there, not because you choose to be there, but because you can be nowhere else. Even if a Westerner decided never to leave Papua New Guinea under any circumstances (a difficult decision to bind on those responsible for you), it would still be a matter of choice. Papua New Guineans have no such choice.

Gifts of pure love are elusive.

MEDITATION

Luke 7:36–50

Week 3

GIFTS OF POISON

13

Destructive Gifts

There have been several hints already that there can be a poisonous side to gifts. On first impression most gifts might appear to be exciting. They are used to show friendship and love. Gifts frequently have an element of surprise. We wrap them carefully to hide their shape. We place them around Christmas trees with a clear warning that they are not to be opened until 25th December. Or we conceal them around the home until the appropriate day arrives.

But not all gifts are gifts of love and not all "gifted" people are forces for good. In German the word *Gift* means not a present but poison. And in English we still talk about someone being "given" poison, being "given" diseases, or even being "given" the sack!

Proverbs sometimes offer warnings about gifts. There is the gentle warning of the proverb which is to be found in many languages, "Don't look a gift-horse in the mouth". By being over-keen to inspect the teeth, and thus the age, of the horse that is being offered as a gift you may fail to appreciate that it is a gift. Then there is the more ominous classical proverb; "I fear the Greeks bearing gifts", or "beware of strangers bearing gifts" as it has sometimes become.

Note, we do not say, "beware of strangers bearing what they are pretending to be gifts, but in reality may be something quite different". This might be the meaning of the proverb – it certainly was in its classical form in the context of the story of the Trojan horse. However in its modern form it might mean that the strangers really do think these are gifts that we will value, but actually they are unwelcome or even bad for us. These are, after all, strangers. They do not know us and they have no idea whether their gifts will please or annoy us, or whether their gifts will help or harm us.

Even gifts within families may have problems. Perhaps the gift is just a token gift – a box of chocolates, a bottle of wine, a familiar scent. Little danger here. And little excitement either. However, perhaps for once we go bananas. On an impulse we spend more generously than usual, possibly too generously. We buy the one we love something expensive and exotic. A day-trip to Paris on Concorde... a white mink coat... a complete luxury edition of the Encyclopaedia Britannica. We are thrilled at our daring and generosity.

Then the doubts begin. That money was really intended to replace the ten-year old car or to repaint the house. It could have bought a less exotic trip to Paris, a cheaper coat *and* a second-hand Encyclopaedia Britannica. Or it could have been given to the Third World. And, in any case, was this an act of spontaneous generosity or just impulsive extravagance? And is she or he going to be thrilled or angry? Will it act as a bond of love? Or will it rather precipitate a lecture on the misuse of fossil fuels, the cruelty behind furs, or the decimation of rain forests? Some gifts do indeed cause resentment and anger.

Gifts can also damage and even destroy people. Because they are unexpected they can induce disorder. Because they are often unusual they can disrupt. Because they are unearned they can also spoil. The theme this week is the destructive side of gifts.

MEDITATION

Genesis 3:1-15

14

Chaos and the Gifted

Of the seven Americans to be awarded the Nobel Prize for Literature five were alcoholics. Eugene O'Neill was already an alcoholic before he became an author. He came from a chronically alcoholic family, which he depicted in his play *Long Day's Journey into Night*. With great effort he finally overcame his alcoholism. But Ernest Hemingway, John Steinbeck, Sinclair Lewis and William Faulkner all died as alcoholics.

Hemingway's life was chaotic at many levels. The macho game hunter, the womanizer, the brawler, the braggart. In Southern Spain at the exquisite little town of Ronda there are photographs of him in the museum attached to its famous bull ring: the celebrated American author in search of excitement and pretending to be a part of this cruel and dangerous "sport", when manifestly his bulk would have presented an easy target to any fighting bull.

Looking through photographs of Hemingway posing for the camera in Spain, on safari in Africa, or basking on some West Indian beach, his bravado appeared to become increasingly desperate. The master of fiction seemed to have become a player in his own worlds of fantasy. The smile for the camera became ever more contrived, perhaps with increasing bleakness descending between shots.

He finally committed suicide, like his father before him, when his brain was so damaged that he could no longer write effectively. Powerful and original "gifts" of writing slowly poisoned by massive alcoholism.

John Steinbeck's genius and personal chaos are both evident in his haunting story *Tortilla Flat*. Through the story the reader soon begins to feel what it was like to be a peasant in Mexico. The hopes and longings of the central characters become real and so does their craving for alcohol. Everything they do to earn money is directed to obtaining more tequila and their ultimate pleasure is to be drunk, totally drunk, to be in a blind alcoholic stupor. Slowly as you read the story you begin to realize that Steinbeck knows their feelings from the inside. It is his craving that these unruly Mexicans voice. Alcohol inspires and eventually destroys his gift for story-telling.

In his magnificent biography of Tolstoy the novelist A. N. Wilson paints a picture of a life constantly on the edge of chaos. Tolstoy's death scene must be amongst the most famous and indeed notorious. Well into his eighties, he tried to escape from his wife, caught pneumonia, and then lay slowly dying in the station master's isolated house at Astapovo.

What is less well known is that the family relationships of this prophet of Christian living had been deeply disturbed for many years. As a young man Tolstoy fought unsuccessfully to control his own promiscuity. Even repeated and highly painful venereal infections from prostitutes did not change his behaviour. And after his marriage he quarrelled massively and repeatedly with his family.

As Wilson points out:

> The life of this author is full of contradictions and puzzles. The paradoxes of Tolstoy are numberless. For instance, this most Russian of novelists was almost entirely influenced not by Russians but by English and French writers. His vision of Christianity owes much more to American Quakers and French rationalists than it does to Russian Orthodox spirituality. And yet he believed himself to be speaking, for much of the time, with the authentic voice of the Russian peasant. There have been many who turned from Tolstoy's later work – his advocacy of political anarchism, for example, or his condemnation of Shakespeare – with something like hatred. Others, inspired by the Christian simplicity of his later writings, have been disillusioned to discover, upon reading about his life, that the great prophet of peace lived in an atmosphere of domestic hatred perhaps unrivalled in the history of matrimony.

The author of *War and Peace* – for many the greatest novel ever written – combined gifts and chaos in a unique and highly contradictory fashion.

The "gifted" in many areas of the arts seem to be especially prone to chaotic and destructive lifestyles, the artist or the actor unable to sustain loving relationships. Vincent van Gogh, lonely and distraught, mutilating himself, poignantly expressing his feelings through his art, and finally committing suicide. Rodin sleeping with countless models. The jazz musicians Fats Waller, Coleman Hawkins and many others, poisoned by drugs or excessive alcohol. Mozart, childish and immature, neglecting his wife and children. Wagner overbearing, arrogant and appallingly anti-Semitic. Schumann descending into insanity. Liszt, even when committed to monastic vows, continuing his old habits of sexual promiscuity.

We are even beginning to admit a bleaker side to some of those who are religiously "gifted". Luther was deeply anti-Semitic. The American theologian Paul Tillich was surprisingly promiscuous. Even the immensely influential Swiss theologian Karl Barth and the American civil rights leader Martin Luther King were by no means conventional in their sexual relationships. Chaos and "giftedness" seem to be closely related.

MEDITATION

Judges 4:12-21

15

An Explanation

Of course not all of those who are considered to be "gifted" have chaotic or destructive lifestyles. There are many writers, artists, musicians and actors who sustain loving and faithful relationships and who avoid drugs or excessive alcohol. "Gifts" are not to be identified with "chaos". Bach led a most ordered and conventional life. Yet those with special gifts do at least seem prone to chaos.

Perhaps it is precisely because gifts are so unusual and unexpected that they tend to disturb and disrupt. Even those who have these gifts frequently feel unable wholly to control them. They appear as "other" and "received" not just to strangers but even to those who are themselves "gifted". Hence the language of "gifts" rather than skills.

The oddity of "gifts" has been reinforced by those studying the gifted in scientific terms. Children with prodigious musical gifts apparently do not on average practise their musical instruments for any longer than other less gifted children. Nor do they typically come from outstandingly musical families. They are just different from other children.

Bach and Mozart did both come from musical families. In Johann Sebastian Bach's case there were at least six generations of musicians in the family. A few of them were famous, especially one of his younger sons, C. P. E. Bach, but most of them were not. They were professional musicians, making a living at the courts of aristocrats, assiduous no doubt in practising their craft, but essentially lacking the elusive "gifts" which Johann Sebastian had in abundance.

Similarly, prodigiously "gifted" chess players can sometimes appear elusive and strange. The reclusive Bobby Fischer is surely amongst the oddest of them all. With a chess rating only recently surpassed by Kasparov, his behaviour whilst world champion in the early 1970s became increasingly eccentric and his exacting requirements more and more puzzling.

At first many people thought that he was simply after more money for appearing in chess matches (by today's standards performance fees were very poor). However, gradually it became clear that he lived in a world of phobias and neuroses. His gifts as a chess player were seemingly not matched by any gifts for coping with public scrutiny or social relationships.

In theory, at least, one might imagine that good chess players would make excellent politicians. They should be able to work out all the possible implications of acting in one way rather than another at national and international levels. Or perhaps they should make excellent military commanders, with their ability to work out complex tactical moves and their knowledge of defence and attack.

In practice, they are seldom particularly good at anything but chess. They are not usually the most talented people intellectually at academic subjects, nor do they necessarily have all the personal skills that are required of politicians. Despite apparent similarities with other areas of life, chess seems to be a remarkably confined game.

Gifts here do not necessarily carry over into the rest of life.

Similarly, gifted academics seldom seem to make particularly gifted politicians. Ironically, professors of politics can be found in most universities and their advice is constantly sought by quality newspapers. Yet few of them actually become politicians themselves, and of those who do very few indeed reach high office. Three out of nine postwar British Prime Ministers never went to university at all, and of those who did only two might have been qualified to become university dons.

There are even scientific reports of individuals who are otherwise severely mentally handicapped yet who are able to achieve astonishing arithmetical or spatial tasks, individuals who can calculate in a flash the day of the week on 14th February 1802, on 21st June 1773, on 2nd April 2163, or whatever ... when most of us have extreme difficulty in working out days for dates just two or three weeks hence.

Again there are apparently individuals who can reproduce exact technical drawings of buildings viewed briefly and just once. Or those who can memorize the positions of hundreds of objects on a tray. Yet most of us can scarcely draw from memory our own homes with any accuracy or remember twenty objects on a tray in party games.

These gifts are not simply unusual. They can appear deeply disturbing. Because conformity is so much more comfortable for most of us for most of the time, they confuse and disturb us. They also put in question our own much more limited "gifts". Furthermore, some of those who are "gifted" seem themselves to be unusually disturbed.

MEDITATION

2 Kings 5

16

Gifts that Poison

In a review of a rather sad biography of Christina Onassis, John Mortimer noted that if you wish to harm a child, give that child plenty of money. However, if you wish to kill, give that child a multi-million annuity. Money, which is essential for survival in our society and which in appropriate amounts can bring freedom to families, in excess can without care soon lead to destruction.

Any parent will be aware of this problem albeit at a more humdrum level. Giving care, protection and love are essential for the well-being of any child. But giving in excess soon spoils and even destroys. The very things that bring well-being can themselves bring ill-being. It is all too easy to spoil children . . . "killing with kindness".

For the year we worked in Papua New Guinea we discovered a new term . . . "mission brat". The origins of this term were not hard to find. Amidst a sea of brown faces and curly hair, usually dark but sometimes ginger, the features of blond Nordic children of Western missionaries made a striking contrast. In rural areas which only occasionally saw Western children, they were always given special attention. Even at a distance we would hear the calls of local children . . . "Come on John, come and play with me" . . . "Hello Sally, come on Sally".

Wherever they went Western children were always assured of adulating friends, giggling at everything they said, and complying with their slightest whims. Small wonder that they soon became petty tyrants. British imperialism writ large in a four-year-old. Perplexed parents soon discovered why other Westerners dubbed them "mission brats".

What really annoyed them most was that the very paternalism which had characterized so many missionaries in the past, and which they had struggled hard to avoid themselves, was now re-surfacing in their own children. Galling in the extreme!

However, it isn't just the special circumstances of Papua New Guinea that cause problems for parents. Going to college can be just as fraught a time for parents and students alike. It is probably good for students to be on limited grants and to learn how to cope with constrained budgets. Local authorities expect parents to make appropriate contributions; yet, if they are too generous with them, they may quickly destroy any training a more limited grant would bring and detract from the sense of freedom that should go with being a student. The natural desire of parents to care and protect can, even in small excess, make students both more vulnerable in later life and extremely resentful in the present. Over-generosity is a risky business.

Again, food is obviously essential for survival and can

often be a source of pleasure and hospitality, but in excess leads to deformity and shortens lives. And alcohol, whilst never essential, for many of us is a pleasure and a means of hospitality, but in excess poisons bodies and wrecks personal relationships. Even air, if breathed in excess, affects consciousness.

It was once quite common to hear the classical proverb "moderation in all things". On this understanding, excess of any kind should be avoided: it is important instead to be moderate in all things. Of course it is not too difficult to reduce this proverb to nonsense, since few would recommend a moderate amount of murder or a moderate amount of bank robberies! Yet there is some obvious good sense in the notion that so many things, including salt, induce health or well-being in moderation but destruction in excess.

Perhaps that is why we have such a strong aversion to "do-gooders". This surely cannot be because we want people to go around doing evil. It isn't the good that do-gooders do that is wrong. Rather it is their paternalism, their inability to listen to our real needs, and their insufferable self-righteousness. Their particular excesses are more to do with pride and overbearance. Doing good in itself must by definition be good.

In short, gifts, intended as gifts of love, in excess or in the wrong contexts, can soon become gifts of poison.

MEDITATION

Matthew 14:1-12

17

Giving Presents

At an everyday level even giving presents can be less than loving. One anthropologist studied present-giving in a traditional village high in the mountains of Spain. The village saw few strangers and at the time had changed little over the years. This was seemingly a stable and settled community of peasant farmers.

To his surprise he discovered that there was an elaborate system of expectations related to gifts in the village. Every bride was expected to give her mother-in-law a certain kind of present, bridegrooms other types of present. Visiting relatives other types again. However, what was most surprising to the outsider was that all of these "gifts" were exactly prescribed and individuals defied village convention at their peril. Presents in this system were no longer spontaneous gifts of love but required donations. They established a hierarchy and gave power to one group over another. They were especially a means of keeping the young in control. The incoming bride or bridegroom from a neighbouring village represented an obvious threat of innovation and change. To control this the villagers colluded in an elaborate pattern of required "gifts".

Even in urban Britain present-giving can be less than loving. Christmas, whilst enjoyed by many, can be a cause of deep pain and depression in others. At a time when society is geared to present-giving, when small children can think of little else for weeks beforehand, and shops are laden with expensive gifts, those at the margins can feel more excluded than ever. Communal present-giving is not much fun for those who are forgotten.

As I watch and enjoy the Sunday School children in our church performing once again the now traditional mixture of Matthew's and Luke's birth stories, I sometimes wonder about those gifts. The astrologers from the East bringing gold, frankincense and myrrh, and we normally assume that these were seen by Matthew as gifts of pure love. But were they?

In our church the heaviest competition amongst the youngest children is to be angels. With whoops of delight they scamper up the aisle to sit on the chancel steps in front of Mary, Joseph and the baby Jesus. Then as angels, and occasionally as fallen angels, they beam to their parents. In our previous church the keenest competition was to be sheep . . . it was after all a deeply rural parish.

As they grow older, and before they can aspire to be Mary or Joseph, the best parts are then considered to be the wee three kings . . . this is a church in the Scottish Borders. And as "kings" they duly bring the "gifts" up the aisle with a mixture of solemnity and levity. These may be "kings" but they are still "gifts" and Christmas for the children involved is self-evidently about gifts.

But suppose these gifts are actually a warning? Just two chapters later in Matthew (4:1-11) the adult Jesus is offered three "gifts" in the wilderness. The voice of Evil tempts him, first with something material, then with supernatural power, and finally with total power over life and death. Perhaps the proverb is right . . . beware of strangers bearing gifts.

A folk tradition has gradually grown around the Christmas story as it is acted out in Sunday School plays and carol services. However even within that tradition there are hints of more sinister elements. That impossible carol "We Three Kings of Orient Are" – impossible because the words and music seldom jell – has come to dictate the meaning of the three "gifts". It has little problem with the first two. Gold is brought "to crown him again – King for ever, ceasing never, over us all to reign". And frankincense "owns a Deity nigh: prayer and praising, all men raising, worship him, God most high". It is the third which presents the problem: "Myrrh is mine, its bitter perfume breathes a life of gathering gloom, sorrowing, sighing, bleeding, dying, sealed in the stone-cold tomb".

This whole folk tradition might come under increasing stress as the year 2000, the Millennium, approaches. At the moment in Britain traditional Christian beliefs appear to be becoming more and more thinly spread. In the religious vacuum once occupied by Sunday Schools and churches a New Age literature is gaining ground. Walk into any High Street bookshop and you are likely to find more books on horoscopes, astrology, the "earth goddess" Gaia, and a series of loosely connected beliefs associated with the New Age Movement, than on Christianity. In this situation of resurgent paganism the three Magi may begin to look less cosy. Perhaps in our rush to make Christmas a household festival we have become blind to what is sometimes the poisonous side of gifts. In Matthew's story there are more than a few hints of this.

As a curate I once tried to incorporate this other side of gifts into a Christmas play. I organized it in the primary school on a new housing estate which I visited each week. Mary and Joseph sat with the baby Jesus in the middle of the stage, but around them was mayhem. I asked the children to act out types of evil which ran counter to the life of Jesus.

With enormous enthusiasm the children acted out scenes of murder, violence and robbery. And Mary and Joseph sat serenely in the middle. It was hardly a traditional Christmas play, but the children seemed to relish it and the parents naturally enjoyed seeing their children acting so enthusiastically. Then it slowly began to dawn on me – it was the violence more than the story which the children were enjoying!

MEDITATION

Matthew 2:1-12

18

Abusing Gifts

Perhaps most sinister of all, "gifts" can be used for evil rather than good. In a sense both Hitler and Stalin were extremely gifted individuals. They clearly had massive powers of leadership. Both had "charisma", as it is sometimes called – interestingly it is the Greek word used in the New Testament for "a spiritual gift". They could control other people in ways that are difficult to understand.

Hitler certainly had immense gifts of oratory and the use of language. He regularly practised his gestures in front of a mirror and had an extraordinary ability to control crowds. He was a master at mass leadership. And Stalin had obvious gifts of organization and a rare ability to identify opportunities for power over other people.

Yet by using these gifts they were responsible between them for killing some fifty million people.

It is frequently claimed that it is religion which has caused so many wars and so much killing in the world. When people make this claim they usually have in mind the troubles in Northern Ireland or the effects of Islamic fundamentalism. Perhaps even the sight of Saddam Hussein praying as the bombs first landed on Baghdad. But we have short memories. Hitler and Stalin, two profoundly anti-religious men, between them caused levels of killing grossly in excess of any other twentieth-century atrocities. Both systematically repressed religious institutions which showed any kind of opposition. Both also used their personal "gifts" in ways which now appear to us as deeply evil, perhaps even satanic.

One of the most unusual studies of life under Hitler looked at the way Jehovah's Witnesses fared in Nazi Germany. The author found that they responded to Hitler more courageously than many in more conventional churches. Hitler in turn hated and vehemently persecuted them. Their jagged beliefs made them refuse to have anything to do with Fascism, and they were quite prepared to die as martyrs. Many of them did, under both Hitler and Stalin.

It is ironic that a religious movement with such a low opinion of the rest of humanity should itself have been so impressive in purely human terms. Hitler and Stalin, in contrast, repeatedly murdered others to protect their own lives. They both ruthlessly used their powerful gifts to intimidate, terrorize and finally to liquidate those who dared to oppose them . . . and countless others besides.

Perhaps all of this is too gross. For most of us the excesses of Hitler or Stalin are appalling aberrations not the stuff of everyday life. Occasionally a psychopath gains power in a heavily armed nation, or like Saddam Hussein devotes a huge slice of his nation's finances to amassing sophisticated weaponry, and the rest of the world quakes. Yet for the most part we are spared such excesses.

More insidious perhaps is the individual with gifts who is admired and praised whilst alive but later exposed as a charlatan or even as a despot, someone who once appeared to be a "hero" but is now unmasked as a villain.

For me the celebrated nineteenth-century explorer Stanley falls into this category. In 1991 it was the one hundred and fiftieth anniversary of his birth, and the despotic side of this Victorian "hero" has now begun to emerge. He is remembered, rather unfairly, by later generations as the one who uttered those inept words, "Dr Livingstone I presume", when he found the missionary/explorer who had been missing in Central Africa for three years. What is less well known is that he was a compulsive liar, paranoid bully, egotist and abysmal imperialist.

His sad origins doubtless contributed to his mercurial character. Henry Morton Stanley was born "John Rowlands" and was the illegitimate son of an alcoholic housemaid. He was deposited in a Welsh workhouse at the age of five and only escaped ten years later to become a cabin boy on a ship going to New Orleans. At the age of eighteen he adopted the same surname as a cotton-broker who acted as his benefactor. He then served in the American

Civil War, first on the side of the South and then on the side of the North, before deserting altogether.

His deeply disturbed early life taught him to survive through deceit and cunning, and he used these "gifts" to great personal advantage in his various journeys. He became a journalist, first on the *Missouri Democrat* covering the war against the Plains Indians and then on the prestigious *New York Herald*. It was whilst writing for this second newspaper at the age of thirty-one that he made his famous and successful journey to find Livingstone.

The boy brought up in extreme poverty was now an international hero. Within two years he was back in Africa undertaking the astonishing feat of circumnavigating Lake Victoria for the first time, thereby establishing the long-debated source of the Nile, and then tracing the Lualaba river via the Congo back into the Atlantic Ocean. In all it took him and those of his party who survived almost three years. In Victorian terms it was one of the most daring explorations ever known.

Two years later he was hired by King Leopold II of Belgium to re-establish the Congo Free State as it was called, although perhaps the term "imperial" might have been more appropriate than "free". He achieved this by taking steamers up the Congo, establishing over twenty garrisoned stations and sometimes filling in ravines to drag his steamers overland. This whole enterprise took a further five years. However, once concluded he was back in Africa within a another two years, this time rescuing an Egyptian satrap who had adopted the name Emin Pasha, involving three dangerous journeys through the Itari forest.

In an age which is now much more suspicious of European colonialism, it is no longer plausible to view these simply as splendid adventures. Modern biographers of Stanley tell a much bleaker story of his appalling cruelty to Africans and of his stubborn disregard for the safety of his companions. His final venture apparently inspired Conrad's *Heart of Darkness*, with its theme of how apparently "civilized" people became corrupted once alone in Africa. Sure in the knowledge of his own racial superiority, Stanley became not a hero but a heartless despot.

Of course it is all too easy to judge others at a distance. The faults of the Victorians are only too obvious to us and doubtless our faults will be equally obvious to future generations. Yet the point of this story is not to sit in judgement on the long-dead Stanley but simply to note that "gifts" can turn sour. Gifts that amaze one generation can appear repulsive to the next.

Gifts can be dangerous.

MEDITATION

Luke 15:11–32

Week 4

GOD-GIVEN

19

God-given Countryside

"I suppose you think you have a God-given right to walk across my land?" If you live in the countryside and have a dog, these words may be horribly familiar.

As soon as the fields are harvested North Northumberland becomes a golden paradise. A decade ago most fields were ploughed in the late autumn and left as brown furrows all winter. Then gradually in the spring they turned green and lush. In late July, and sometimes not until August, they turned from green to golden yellow. Then massive combine harvesters moved in. For a week or two all was noise, and constant scratching from the harvest midges. But afterwards the countryside was gloriously open to people and dogs.

Today the pattern has changed slightly. Winter barley and hardier crops mean that we are no longer surrounded by brown earth all winter. Fields are often ploughed soon after harvesting and then planted almost immediately. By October they are already green, and remain so throughout the long winter. They look better and doubtless yield better, but the time for walking dogs is distinctly shorter. And in any case it clashes with the release of innumerable half-tame pheasants, scurrying along the hedgerows, unsure about flying, and standing resolutely in the path of people and cars. The local farmers and gamekeepers naturally want to protect land, birds and animals. The rest of us would prefer to roam freely – the sheer thrill of walking across endless fields once the crop is harvested and before ploughing starts; agricultural countryside returned to open moorland. Instead of river paths or walks along tarmac, for once it becomes possible to range across one field after the next. That is, until you hear those words again!

Because I like to walk at dusk I must appear especially sinister. Whatever the time of year North Northumberland is particularly haunting as it grows dark. Walking along the path on the winding river banks, or in autumn across the open fields, it is rare to meet other people or dogs. Quite alone and in the midst of nowhere dogs and owners commune with nature. Sometimes we battle strongly against the prevailing wind from the west. At other times we are crunching through ice and snow. Or sniffing the wet leaves and grass between spring showers. And just occasionally we are walking through warm, serene countryside.

For the dogs these walks involve a ceaseless attempt to disturb every pheasant and rabbit within range. For me they mean listening to the sounds of dogs and birds, smelling the evening air, being at one with bracing elements, and endlessly thinking.

"I suppose you think you have a God-given right to walk across my land?" The words soon bring any communing with nature to an abrupt halt. This is poaching country and a man with two springer spaniels must be challenged. Fortunately this is also a community where all are known, and apologies are soon made on both sides.

But perhaps the phrase has deeper resonances than a simple challenge to trespassers or poachers. It is meant to be a warning and a reminder about who owns or rents the land. The anxious gamekeeper must protect the pheasants for the winter shoot, and the farmer is concerned about sheep escaping or about his prize cattle becoming infected unintentionally by earth trampled from a neighbouring farm. Yet language about God-given rights also carries within it a hint of something else.

One of my favourite fields is known locally as "the haugh" – pronounced "hoff" but with a guttural Northumbrian "ghhhh". The haugh is surrounded on three sides by a medium-size river, which at times becomes large and dangerous. Forty years ago a villager's only son drowned nearby, attempting to brave the river in full flood. The hidden power of the river has never been forgotten since then.

The twenty acres of the haugh are never ploughed but always kept as a rough meadow for hardy northern sheep or occasionally for cattle. In the middle are three ancient wych elms and in the near distance stands Cheviot, capped with snow even in June. From the end of the haugh and looking backwards two fourteenth-century castles can be seen standing guard against bygone Scottish enemies, one in ruins now and the other masquerading as an eighteenth-century mansion. This is Border Country.

Joined ironically to the ruined castle is the shell of an old Scottish Presbyterian church. The minister there is still remembered half a century later with a mixture of affection and sadness. For forty years, summer or winter, he bathed in the river. He was a hard, kindly man, living on a pittance, retiring in his eighties with his congregation all but vanished. A village once teeming with life now shrunk to a handful of pensioners. Even his wife left him, taking most of the furniture with her. She had had enough. And when the old man finally gave up, the church closed and two centuries of Scottish churchgoing on this piece of English soil came to an end.

On the banks in spring and summer oyster-catchers shriek, distracting the dogs from their nests. In winter flocks of arctic geese engage in what might fancifully be seen as synchronized swirling, always in V-formations and constantly calling to each other in rich musical tones. Rabbits scamper and wild ducks pretend to be lame ducks to confuse the dogs. And all is well with the world. Whatever the political crisis, whatever the problems at work, whatever the weather . . . all is well with the world. The haugh is truly God-given.

Trudging around the haugh I have written many books, some of them transferred to paper but most of them not. The dogs have listened patiently to many of the ideas they contain . . . wisely never passing comment. The sheep have never ever objected. And only once have frisky bullocks given chase to dogs and aspirant author alike. Who knows what creative ideas were lost to the world that day?

As evening descends, the vast Northumbrian sky often glows orange and then purple. Sometimes after rain the setting sun breaks through in the sort of shafts usually found only in children's paintings. At all times the colours of the grass and river are muted greens and browns and greys. North Northumberland is never overstated. In June faint sunlight lingers almost to midnight, but in December the same walks must be finished some seven hours earlier. Summer or winter the haugh digs deep into the bones. This is hard, raw countryside. But, most important of all, it is God-given.

MEDITATION

Psalm 136:1-9

20

Land as God-given

The Bible is steeped in the idea that land properly belongs to God. In what is sometimes called the Holiness Code it is God who finally owns all land, and it is God who promises and then gives land to people for temporary safekeeping.

So in Deuteronomy the voice of God says to Moses:

> The Lord your God is bringing you to a good land, a land with streams, springs, and underground waters gushing out in valley and hill, a land with wheat and barley, vines, fig trees, and pomegranates, a land with olive oil and honey. It is a land where you will never suffer any scarcity of food to eat, nor want for anything, a land whose stones are iron ore and from whose hills you will mine copper. When you have plenty to eat, bless the Lord your God for the good land he has given you" (Deuteronomy 8:7–10).

Of course this is a rosy, idealized picture. The author in Deuteronomy glosses over the important fact that this land already belongs to someone else. God appears to take sides, and the Canaanites and others are all too often regarded as "the enemy" who must be dispossessed of their land. But in theory, at least, the Israelites are reminded that they are stewards rather than owners of the land. The land belongs properly to God . . . not to Canaanites, not to Israelites, but to God.

There are various reminders of this important ideal in

the earliest books of the Bible. Later in the same book of Deuteronomy Moses is depicted commanding the Israelites to place in a basket the first part of each crop and to take it to the place of worship. They are then to recite all the good things that God has done for them, finishing with the words:

> He has brought us to this place and gave us this land, a land flowing with milk and honey. Now I have brought here the firstfruits of the soil which you, LORD, have given to me" (Deuteronomy 26:9–10).

Immediately following are detailed instructions about the Israelites' duty to give also to the priests, to aliens, to orphans and to widows. None must be forgotten, especially the weak and the defenceless. Land and the various fruits of the land are gifts from God, gifts which must also be shared with those in need.

Further, in what the book of Leviticus terms the Jubilee Year, servants and land must once more be free. Every fiftieth year was to be a Jubilee Year: "Hallow the fiftieth year and proclaim liberation in the land for all its inhabitants" (Leviticus 25:10). Here the Israelites are reminded that "no land is to to be sold outright" because it properly belongs to God (Leviticus 25:23). Land may look as if it belongs to individuals, but in reality it is God-given and in the end it still belongs to God.

Whether the Jubilee Year laws were ever practised is open to considerable doubt. Perhaps they represented an ideal which the priestly writer deemed should be the case, rather than a record of what in reality occurred. They were a utopian goal, always beyond reach, but none the less pointing in a direction to move.

Whatever . . . the Jubilee Year laws respond to an experience which many will have had. Walking across freshly harvested fields, hiking across open moorland, or gazing out to sea on a still, clear day, it is not difficult to believe that people are just stewards. The earth and the sea seem indeed to be God-given.

MEDITATION

Deuteronomy 26

21

Life as God-given

It is at moments of fragility that we can become most conscious that life is God-given – birth and death especially. I wrote earlier about the fragility that parents often experience when their first child is born. Many will feel that their baby really is God-given. After all, they did so little to produce it. Similar feelings are also common near death.

When I was a curate I and others regularly took communion to a hundred-year-old woman. Everybody around her was thrilled that she had reached a century, had received her telegram from the Queen, and had retained her faculties. She herself was not quite so convinced. She was gentle and kind with the young curates. Yet when it came to the intercessions in the service she always interrupted. "Pray that I may be taken", she insisted. I was never sure what prayer I was supposed to use for this request!

For her life was clearly God-given. The next life would be a distinct improvement. And it was for God to effect this change. It was certainly not for human beings to do so. Whereas some of those weary of life might say to their doctor, "Please end my life", she in contrast said to her priest, "Pray that I may be taken".

Bewildered as I was by this request, I could still glimpse something of the experience of God-givenness that lay behind it. Having reached the age of one hundred she had lost all of her friends. Having never married she had also lost all of her immediate family. She had seen enough of this life and wished to move on to the next one. Untroubled by the doubts of the youngsters who surrounded her, she was certain that life is God-given and that it returns in due course to God. So it was only natural that she should require the young curates to remind God that her return was overdue.

Of course I saw things differently. I still valued her as a person. I was in awe of her longevity and felt humble in the presence of her faith. Also, I had no idea what words I should use to comply with her request. In the end the familiar words of the liturgy were those we used together. Through them she could make her prayers and I could make mine.

In the company of the very elderly it is not difficult to feel the presence of God. It is well established that belief in afterlife grows stronger amongst the elderly. Of course this could be because they belong to a generation in Britain which was more intimately involved in the churches. Yet it seems true also of countries such as the United States, where churches have remained comparatively strong or where they have even grown over the course of this century.

Perhaps it has more to do with the life-cycle of individuals. It may be natural for teenagers to be sceptical; and it may be natural for young parents to begin to feel more fragile and responsible for the new life they have produced. So perhaps it is also natural that the elderly should begin to wonder about life in God, about the possibility of the love of God extending beyond this life. As we all grow older so we change. And perhaps it is right that we should do so. Wisdom with age.

Whatever the reason, as a young priest I was conscious of my privileged role. Not for me the bedpans, the bedsores, the tantrums, and the many lapses from grace. Instead, in the presence of those near the end of their lives, I was privileged to be allowed to listen, to learn of worlds that were passing, and to pray.

Every Christmas Day and Easter Sunday I take communion to an old people's home just down the road from our church. At one time it was a grand country mansion. The stables were packed with hunters and the kitchens thronged with servants. It had a reputation for wild parties and high living. Today it is a private nursing home, run for profit, but not without care.

The communion service must be squeezed into the hour between the early and later services at church. Often the residents are confused, talking and singing in the wrong places. But at the Lord's Prayer all the lips start to move together. We sing a carol or an Easter hymn or two – or perhaps more accurately I sing and they follow – but when it comes to the Lord's Prayer we all pray together. Memories, almost buried, briefly return. Finally, we share Communion together – Anglicans, Scottish Presbyterians, Methodists, or whatever – I never fail to feel the presence of God.

Some moments in this life seem to be truly God-given.

MEDITATION

Psalm 90

22

A Fleeting Gift

When a close friend or someone we love dies young it is common to feel anger and perplexity. "Why did she have to die?" "Why has God done this to me?"

As a young curate I was always tempted to answer these questions. All the years of theological training and wrestling with the problem of innocent suffering seemed to be geared for these occasions. Of course there were mysteries here, and there was no easy answer to the paradox of a world created by a loving God in which there is still innocent suffering. Yet there were also confusions. And those numb with grief might surely be helped by clearing away some of these confusions.

Slowly I learned otherwise. People in the midst of grief need love and patience not logic. They may also need to pray, even when they are still angry with God or feel confused about whether they believe in God at all. The gentle presence of a priest who can attempt to share a small part of their grief and hold their hand in prayer is worth more than a plethora of gifted theologians.

Perhaps what most helped me to understand this for myself was the death of my best man. He was a young priest of remarkable gifts.

I first met Rod at theological college. Like me he was single-minded and kept slightly apart from the crowd. His passion was rock-climbing and cycle-riding. My passion was theology and playing the trumpet. But he respected theology and I respected rock-climbing, so we spent hours in mutual instruction.

Rod was stocky and muscular and had a reputation for friendliness and heroic feats. One weekend he cycled to Paris and back and the next he was climbing in the Avon Gorge. Once he took me climbing. He chose a twenty-foot stone wall of a disused railway bridge to teach me the first clumsy lessons in crampons and pitons and ropes and footholds.

I was terrified. Vigorous exercise was one thing, but this was appalling. Each time I returned to the ground my legs shook uncontrollably. Rod just laughed. The theologian humbled!

At other times we argued about theology. He was a fan of the radical German theologian Rudolf Bultmann. Here for Rod was a tough-minded theologian who was facing the hardest problems and searching for a credible route through them. For many of us Bultmann was too sceptical.

Not for Rod. Bultmann's work allowed him to combine a deep personal piety with a rugged critical method – exactly what Rod found in mountain climbing. Exhausting, demanding climbs combined with moments of sheer exhilaration alone at the top of a mountain.

Some weeks after the wedding Rod came to see us at our little flat in Thornton Heath. He had worked in the parish all day, changed into his scruffy clothes, and travelled down from the Midlands on the last train. Unsure of the night buses in south London he decided to walk the last few miles, carrying his belongings in a battered hold-all.

"Excuse me *sir*. Just where do you think you are going?" Two policemen had stopped their patrol car to question this obvious burglar carrying a bag all but marked "swag". Without waiting for a reply they asked to inspect the contents of the bag. The odd clampon and piton began to emerge, together with a torch and a rope. Only the crow-bar was missing.

"Can I ask what your business is, *sir*?"

Rod explained courteously that he was a clergyman.

Now this was not the most convincing answer that he could have given. So they proceeded to search the rest of the bag, doubtless looking for the loot. It was only when they came to the last two items that they began to have serious doubts. Always pious, Rod had packed his battered Bible and Prayer Book to say Evensong on the train journey down.

Clearly confused by this the policemen decided to accompany him to his alleged destination. Our first intimation was a knock at the door at midnight and a policeman asking whether we had a "clergyman" friend coming to visit us. Then out from the police-car stepped Rod, beaming as always, and immensely proud of the free lift he had secured.

I was best man at his wedding three years later. He was thrilled to be married. It was a blazing summer day and everyone was excited and delighted for Rod and his young bride. Within months he was dead. He used his gifts to become a chaplain and instructor at an outward-bound centre. Then on the simplest of climbs he slipped, fell forty feet, and was killed instantly.

His friends and family felt utterly numb. I have some of the letters we wrote to each other, and each time I read them I can still feel the pain and loss. He had *so* much to offer. He was tough and pious. He would have used his favourite epithet to describe the words I am writing now . . . "grot". He could have led other youngsters to faith. He had a ministry full of promise. Yet he was killed . . . and killed in a stupid, idiotic accident.

Then through the numbness something else began to emerge. I began to feel gratitude. Those closest to him also wrote, despite their pain, of their gratitude for sharing his life however briefly. And these feelings have continued. I still feel gratitude. Echoes of his gifts remain.

Life, even fleeting life, can be seen as God-given.

MEDITATION

Ecclesiastes 7:1-13.

23

The Beginnings of Life

Religious people have been in the forefront of those cam-
paigning against current abortion laws. We are certainly
not united on this difficult issue. Some believe that the law
at present is the lesser of two evils. Others believe that it
is morally repugnant and, what is more important here,
that it treats human life as less than God-given.

Orthodox Jews, many Roman Catholics and some from
other churches, have led a series of political campaigns
to change the 1968 Abortion Act. Groups of otherwise
conservative religious people, who might normally argue
that "religion should keep out of politics", have become
highly politicized. Why is this?

One reason is surely that seeing life as "God-given",
rather than as just "given", adds an extra seriousness to
the way we treat life. This planet is no longer seen as some
kind of fluke, with life, even human life, a chance product
of that fluke. If life really is God-given, then it is invested
with meaning. Gratitude and a sense of responsibility
might seem to be amongst the most appropriate human
responses to such a gift.

I will return to this later. For the moment it is sufficient
to notice that regarding life as "God-given" can change
our whole perspective. A new depth emerges.

Doubtless this does not "solve" the immensely difficult
issue of framing laws on abortion. We may still reluctantly
conclude (as I do) that legal abortions are less damaging
than illegal abortions, that they prevent deaths in women

who would otherwise resort to back-street abortionists. But we cannot treat human life in any form as without value. If it is God-given it does have value.

Perhaps at a practical level it is this which most distinguishes those who believe in God from those who don't. It is clearly not the case that all those who believe in God are anti-abortion, whereas those who don't are pro-abortion. The secular regime of Ceauşescu was fiercely anti-abortion – in the interests of increasing the population of Romania – and resulted in appalling levels of back-street septic abortions. Manifestly divisions on this issue are more complicated than that. Rather it seems to be the case that those who have a deep faith in God tend to deny themselves certain kinds of argument.

So, in the secular debate about abortion it is sometimes held that abortions are merely the removal of unwanted tissue. It is up to the woman, and to the woman alone, to decide whether she wishes to retain this part of her body. If she chooses to have an abortion as if it were just a growth, then that is entirely up to her. Doctors should simply do as they are told.

Expressed in this way, I suspect that most religious people will feel uneasy. If life is God-given, then it cannot properly be regarded simply as "unwanted tissue" or as nothing but a part of a woman's body. As the foetus becomes more recognizably human, then most of us begin to have qualms about regarding it in non-moral terms. We may still believe that abortions, especially in the first trimester, are justifiable. Yet we do so on other grounds . . . care for the woman involved, for the family, and perhaps for the future children.

Few even in secular society are prepared to justify the

practices of the ancient Romans. Exposing babies once born is thought by all but a few to be morally wrong. Notoriously we disagree with each other about the cut-off point for justifiable abortions ... twelve weeks, eighteen weeks, twenty-four weeks, twenty-eight weeks. Yet most of us do have a cut-off point. Most recognize that at some point, usually well before actual birth, this is a human life.

And for many of us it is also a God-given life.

MEDITATION

Isaiah 45:5–13

24

An Objection

There is an obvious objection that can be made to all of this. If everything is regarded as "God-given" and is thus invested with value, does this also apply to the malaria virus or to the AIDS virus?

There are some people who have argued that the AIDS virus is indeed God-given – it is a punishment sent by God. AIDS in the West has spread through human sin. First it attacked the gay community and now it is insidiously infecting the promiscuous heterosexual community.

People have sinned against God and he in turn has punished them through this devastating virus.

I have always thought this to be dangerous nonsense, as it suggests a very inept picture of God. God sends the AIDS virus to punish the sexually promiscuous or mainline drug abusers – yet in the process he also manages to give AIDS to babies, to haemophiliacs, to rape victims and to the spouses of those who are HIV-positive. Just at a time when we are beginning to expect our military to target weapons rather than people, and to eschew the mass civilian bombing that so disfigured the Second World War, we have invented a picture of God spreading AIDS indiscriminately amongst the innocent and indulgent alike.

What an extraordinarily incompetent God that would be! It would also be very different from the image of God visible in Christ. At the heart of the Christian faith is not a brutal God acting as some tyrant to control human sin, but a God sharing our suffering on the cross. God as the crucified God, rather than God as the heavenly despot.

Fortunately this vengeful picture of God using AIDS as a punishment has been presented by only a handful of churches. Many others have been stimulated to work for those with AIDS and to emphasize pastoral care rather than moral judgements. However much we might feel distressed at sexual promiscuity or drug-abuse, confronted with those who are already HIV-positive we soon realize that the time for moralizing at them is long past. Just as Jesus cared especially for those regarded by his society as outcasts, we in turn must act similarly today.

Nevertheless, a dilemma remains. There is much innocent suffering in the world which is not caused, even indirectly, through human actions. The malaria virus, for instance, has destroyed many lives over the centuries and seems to have brought little benefit to the world. Is that God-given too?

Again, in the previous chapter I looked at gifts of poison in several different forms. Are these also to be regarded as God-given? Why do we regard some "gifts" as gifts of love and others as gifts of poison?

Implied in all of these questions is a deeper question about means of discrimination, about means of deciding whether something truly is God-given or not. The very distinctions that I have been making so far between different kinds of gifts imply this. Without some standard these distinctions soon collapse. And if they collapse then gifts – poisonous, loving, or whatever – may appear morally indistinguishable.

It would be foolish in the extreme to imagine that everything in the world can be explained. Who knows, or perhaps will ever know, whether a world could have been created which contained no malaria viruses? Sometimes people glibly claim that a God of love could have created a different world, a world without suffering. How do they know?

What we can know is surely far more limited than that. Talk about the world as a whole, whether to prove or to disprove the existence of a loving God, seems to me to be thoroughly misplaced. It presumes too much, far too much. What we know is rather that some parts of life appear meaningful to us and others not. In some forms of behaviour we see goodness and in others not. In some experiences we seem to encounter the presence of God and in others not.

Perhaps that is sufficient. I suspect that most people find prayer a far more convincing way of knowing that God exists than arguments about the origins or purpose of the universe. Perhaps before the age of Darwin it seemed plausible to believe that the natural world had a "purpose" which should be obvious to all thinking people. But frankly I doubt even this. Surely life has always appeared puzzling – a mixture of pain and pleasure, of sadness and happiness, of well-being and ill-being.

The Bible doesn't contain grand theories about the universe so much as stories about human encounters with God. Jesus in the first three gospels tells parables and points to God's work in the world. He doesn't engage in philosophy or provide definitive arguments about the existence of God or about the ways of the universe. He beckons, warns and encourages. He seldom argues or proves. Even miracles are used to point rather than to prove. Above all he knows the Father in prayer.

For the Christian it is finally in Christ we can see that the gifts of God are gifts of love not poison. Christ as himself God-given – the theme for next week – shapes our very understanding of gifts, of people being gifted, and of the world being given. In Christ certain features of the everyday world become especial signs of a loving God. Gifts of bread and wine take on new meaning in our search for what God is really like.

MEDITATION

Job 38

Week 5

GIFTS IN CHRIST

25

New Depth

Once gifts are seen as "God-given" they take on a new depth. Secular language about things being "given" and about people being "gifted", originally borrowed from a religious context, is transformed back into religious language. In the process, it takes on a new seriousness.

This is a depth and seriousness which is shared by Jews, Christians and Muslims, who all believe in a world that is created by a loving God. We may not always behave as if we do. For centuries we have squabbled, fought and sometimes killed each other. In the name of our "God" we have ridiculed and denounced each other.

Yet in our better moments we remember that we have a common faith in one God, the giver of life and all that is. And we remember that it is God who gives shape and meaning and depth to our lives. The given and the gifted alike are seen in the context of the Divine Giver.

Of course it is possible to use the secular language of gifts without making these religious connections. Perhaps for most of the time many do just that. Religious language is borrowed to denote secular experience and then its religious resonances are forgotten. Or, if they are fleetingly remembered, they are effectively ignored for nine-tenths of the time.

In many Western cultures even the word "God" is used repeatedly and without giving much offence simply to denote surprise. "Oh, my God . . ." has for long been merely a cultural habit even for the pious in France. And in modern Britain it has lost much of the sting it might have had a generation ago. Personally I do still baulk at the term "Jesus Christ" being used as a means of abuse. But I doubt if those who use it in this way mean to give offence.

Instead, if people wish to give extreme offence it is crude sexual terms, rather than religious language, that they most frequently use today. Or perhaps it is obscene gestures. Stuck in rush-hour traffic jams and with tempers become frayed early in the morning, it is quite common to see smartly dressed men and women using fingers and arms in obscene gestures. *That* is intended to give offence. And it does.

In contrast, swearwords with religious origins now have considerably less bite. They have been taken into the secular world and have lost their power to shock or prompt. They seldom annoy and they no longer point most listeners to anything sacred. They have become religious fossils.

It is not so much the words "gifted" and "given" which are interesting. Rather it is the everyday experiences that still lurk behind these words. What I have tried to argue is that gifts, even apparently secular gifts, are odder than might at first appear. It is this oddness which might prompt us to explore religious language. And it is this oddness which receives new depth in religious traditions.

None the less, little has been said up to now in this book which is distinctively Christian. This has been deliberate. My aim is to show that by exploring the language of everyday experience at depth, we can make fresh connections with Christian belief. By doing this we can begin to see that faith really does relate to the everyday world. It can add unexpected depths to everyday experience.

The starting point for this discovery is the simple observation that everyday experience of "gifts" can be highly disturbing. Those who seem especially "gifted" can both attract and repel. "Gifts" can become poisonous and can be disastrously misused. Even the term "God-given" can become highly judgemental.

However in the Christian story "gifts" take on new meanings. If the notion of the "God-given" gives a new seriousness to our secular language, gifts in Christ offer Christians a crucial means of discrimination. In a confused and often perplexing world, Christians believe that Christ gives light. Christ can be the means of distinguishing gifts of love from gifts of poison.

MEDITATION

John 6:25-35

26

Christ as God-given

A central theme running through different parts of the New Testament is that Christ is himself a "gift". He is God-given and he gives his life for us. And, what is more, God's action in Christ has direct implications both for the way we see gifts and for our own "giving".

All of these ideas – God gives Christ, Christ gives his

life, Christ can give shape to our lives, and we in turn must give our lives – are linked together in 1 John. "This is the witness: God has given us eternal life, and this life is found in his Son" (5:11). And, "This is how we know what love is: Christ gave his life for us. And we in turn must give our lives for our fellow-Christians" (3:16).

There is a powerful logic running through this epistle. It is a Christ-centred logic. Christ enables us both to see God more clearly and to give direction and purpose to our own lives. Thus, to know Christ is already to know God. And to know Christ is also to know ourselves. The love of God in Christ tells us about what God is like. It also tells us about what we should be like. In a confused and confusing world, the love of God in Christ offers a witness.

Or, to express this slightly differently, in a world containing gifts of poison as well as gifts of love, the love of God in Christ offers a path. It offers a means of discriminating between poison and love.

Now I am conscious that I am introducing new language at this point, language drawn from religious traditions. It is language which needs some unpacking if we are to learn to talk to those on the edges of faith. For example, what does it mean to say that "God gave his only Son"? Christians use such language so often that we are in danger of forgetting that it is at best indirect language. All four words that follow the word "God" are used indirectly.

They are first and foremost words that derive from everyday life and are used only with some difficulty about God. We can do no other. Strictly speaking, God as God must be beyond human words. Trying to capture the infinite in words that are patently all too finite is bound to be a losing battle.

I suppose that human beings could simply invent words for God which have no link with human experience. They could, but they clearly wouldn't mean very much. They would be little more than noises – although in a moment I will maintain that there is place for religious noises in worship. Yet to have meaning words must obviously relate to experience and the problem is simply that experience is always too constrained to depict God in anything but the most partial terms.

There is a well known Indian story which tries to convey this. Three blind men attempt to describe what an elephant is like to each other through touch alone. One grabs the trunk and describes the elephant as being like a fat snake. Another gets hold of a leg and describes the elephant as being like a tree. The third grapples with the tail and thoroughly disagrees with his companions. Because the elephant is obviously so much larger than any of them, they naturally get a very partial idea through touch alone. And so, says the story, with human words groping for God.

So when we depict God as "King" or "Shepherd" or "Lover" we are taking words from everyday experience and stretching them to refer to God. God has some of the properties of a "King" or a "Shepherd" or a "Lover" . . . only more so, much more so. And when we say that God is "mighty" or "knowing", we qualify these terms with the word "all". God is all-mighty and all-knowing. Instinctively we expand language almost to breaking point to give a glimpse of the mysteries of God.

Similarly, when Christians say that Christ is the "Son"

of God we are again stretching language. Sons are produced by fathers and mothers in the everyday world. They are certainly not eternal. Instead, in the context of Christ, the word "Son" is used to capture something of the special relationship that all of the New Testament writers believe existed between Jesus and God. Like a father and a son . . . only more so, much more so.

Even the word "his" indicates that God is personal rather than simply impersonal, not that God is male. It may seem odd to many Christians today to talk about God in female terms, but there is no reason why we should not. And parts of the Old Testament do just that – most strikingly in Proverbs chapter 8.

What is meant by saying that "God gave his only Son" is that in Christ God takes the initiative. This is not simply a good man, someone to copy, it is a focused action of God. Of course, I am still using indirect language. There is no way of avoiding this (interestingly scientists have the same problem when talking about reality at the smallest and largest levels – which cannot be pictured literally).

Indeed, Christians are those people who believe that they can learn about God by looking at Christ. In Christ God can be seen reaching out to us. In Christ we can see God's true gift of love. Or, to express this another way, God giving of himself to us.

Christ as God-given.

MEDITATION

1 John 3:13-18

27

Gifts around Christ

When you start to notice gifts – as by now you surely will – the gospel stories appear to be punctuated by gifts.

There are the gifts mentioned earlier. In Matthew the Magi in an act of worship bring gifts to the new born baby and in Luke and Matthew the evil one in the wilderness offers to give Jesus the whole world if only Jesus will worship him. Perhaps this is a link that Matthew intends to make. In Luke it stands on its own. However, both recognize in their wilderness stories that "gifts" can indeed be gifts of poison.

There are hints elsewhere that gifts of poison can, sometimes with difficulty, be turned into gifts of love. In both Matthew and Luke, as well as the earlier gospel, Mark, a rich man is told by Jesus to give away his possessions if he wishes to be a disciple. There are fascinating differences of detail between the three versions of the story which tell the careful reader much about the particular emphasis of each of the gospel writers. In Matthew alone he is described as "young", and in Luke alone he is a "ruler".

Mark has vivid personal details missing in the other two gospels: the stranger "ran up" to Jesus "kneeling before him", and Jesus in turn "looked at him, his heart warmed to him". And in Mark the rich man is told bluntly by Jesus:

"Go, sell everything you have, and give to the poor, and

you will have treasure in heaven; then come and follow me" (Mark 10:21).

Matthew softens the blow slightly. Here the man is told to sell "your possessions". In a world of belongings, Matthew perhaps feels the same dilemma as we do. Total giving seems just too risky.

But whatever the differences, the outcome is the same in all three gospels. This is a man of considerable possessions who would like to follow Jesus, but who finally prefers these possessions. In the last resort it is material gifts that take preference in his life over gifts of the Spirit.

In Luke and Matthew, again, the prayer that Jesus teaches his disciples asks that it should be God who gives us bread. In Matthew's words:

> Our Father in heaven,
> may your name be hallowed;
> your kingdom come,
> your will be done,
> on earth as in heaven.
> Give us today our daily bread
> (*Matthew 6:9-11*).

Much controversy surrounds those familiar words "daily bread". The Greek word that is translated "daily" here is so rare that its meaning is still unclear despite much work by scholars. It could indeed mean "daily" and be a reference to the food which is vital for our survival. Many people will understand it this way. Yet it could have the more elusive meaning "for tomorrow". If this were the case it would be a prayer longing for God's future promises, longing for what is sometimes termed the heavenly banquet, God's future Kingdom tasted in advance in Jesus.

Perhaps it is good to be reminded in this most familiar of all prayers that God's "gifts" in Christ are a mixture of illumination and mystery. They start with the everyday – in this case that most basic of foodstuff, bread – but then they point beyond to mysteries glimpsed but not captured. Bread is bread, but for Christians it is also a symbol of the body of Christ.

In each of these three gospels Jesus gives thanks at the Last Supper as he breaks the bread and takes up the cup and then gives them to his disciples. Gifts of love are interweaved with gifts of poison in the story. Present at the Supper is Judas Iscariot, and immediately before their accounts of this Supper each of the three gospel writers recounts the story of his receiving a gift of money to betray Jesus. This time it is perhaps Luke who is the most vivid:

> Then Satan entered into Judas, who was called Iscariot, one of the Twelve; and he went to the chief priests and temple guards to discuss ways of betraying Jesus to them. They were glad and undertook to pay him a sum of money. He agreed, and began to look for an opportunity to betray him to them without collecting a crowd (Luke 22:3-6).

Playwrights have often speculated about Judas Iscariot's motive. Was it power, misplaced idealism, political ambitions . . . ? Frankly there is no conceivable way of telling. Luke seems to attribute it to that commonplace vice . . . greed. Of all the gospel writers Luke is the most conscious of poverty and of the corrupting properties of wealth. So here again it appears to be money – that essen-

111

tial commodity for daily living in any complex society – acting as a gift of poison.

The interweaving of gifts of love and poison also characterizes the earliest version of the Last Supper, that provided by Paul in 1 Corinthians. It is ironic that this highly treasured account appears to have been prompted by the bad behaviour of some in the young congregation at Corinth. Paul accuses them of greed and gross insensitivity even when they come together to celebrate the Lord's Supper:

> The result is that when you meet as a congregation, it is not the Lord's Supper you eat; when it comes to eating, each of you takes his own supper, one goes hungry, and another has too much to drink. Have you no homes of your own to eat and drink in? Or are you so contemptuous of the church of God that you shame its poorest members? What can I say? Can I commend you? On this point, certainly not! (1 Corinthians 11:20-22).

Then, having roundly ticked them off, Paul presents the earliest account of the Last Supper:

> For the tradition which I handed on to you came to me from the Lord himself: that on the night of his arrest the Lord Jesus took bread, and after giving thanks to God broke it and said: "This is my body, which is broken for you; do this in memory of me." In the same way, he took the cup after supper, and said: "This cup is the new covenant sealed by my blood. Whenever you drink it, do this in memory of me" (1 Corinthians 11:23-25).

The one who "gives" his life to be betrayed, mocked and crucified is surrounded by "gifts" at every stage of the story that each gospel writer presents.

In the final gospel, which puzzlingly has no direct account of the Last Supper, there is the evocative story of the risen Jesus taking bread and fish and "giving" it to the disciples on the shore of Lake Tiberias. John skilfully links the whole of his gospel: with the story of the Wedding Feast at Cana-in-Galilee at the beginning; that of the Feeding of the Five Thousand in the middle; and that on the shores of Tiberias at the end. In each Jesus gives the food and/or wine of life. Those early Christians reading John would not have been slow to make the connections here with the Eucharist.

MEDITATION

John 6:1-15

28

Gifts of Tongues

I had seen people "speaking in tongues" on television but had never been to a service which featured the phenomenon. To be honest I was not much impressed with the sensationalism apparent on the television. All too often the cameras tended to focus upon people close to hysteria, pouring out their feelings in what seemed to be invented baby-language.

Then I spoke at the National Conference of the British Jesuits, some of the most powerful brains amongst British Catholics gathered together under one roof, listening to a series of lectures and discussions.

I suppose it could have been a very intimidating experience. Jesuits are notorious both for their brains and for some of their sharp intellectual controversies. In the event I was flattered to be asked to speak to them and much impressed with their friendliness and courtesy. If I had feared in advance the reception my lecture might get – it was laced with some rather blunt sociological observations – the reality was very different. Stereotypes can be highly misleading.

After the lecture they invited me to join them in worship. Of course I agreed. But then they told me that I had to choose. There were three separate services: one was traditional, one was quiet, and the third was noisy. Since I had never heard of a "noisy" service before, the sociologist in me made the third irresistible. It sounded too good to be missed.

The person conducting – perhaps orchestrating would be a more appropriate term – the noisy service explained the pattern of what was to follow. We were to sit in a large circle. There would be some singing, some readings and some prayer. But during the prayers, if people felt moved, they were encouraged to speak in tongues.

I waited with great interest. At last I was to find out what all this "speaking in tongues" was about. Like some anthropologist studying a little-known tribe, I was to see at first hand this strange form of religious behaviour. If I had been asked in advance I would never have predicted that it would be here amongst Jesuits of all people that I would first make these observations.

When we finally came to the prayers one or two of the Jesuits did start to speak in tongues. More accurately, they began to sing in tongues. No hysteria. No shouting or ranting. No volatile displays of religious emotion. Just quietly sitting, intoning prayers, in sounds rather than words.

My prejudices instantly evaporated. Nobody claimed that this was some exotic new tongue. There was no suggestion that those speaking in tongues were talking fluently in some foreign language which they had never learned before. Nobody argued that they were imparting new knowledge or (worse still) predictions about the future. There was nothing in the least magical about their speaking in tongues. It was simply prayer.

And why not? Prayer can take many forms. For the child it is typically asking for this and that ... a long list of family members, pets and others to protect. For the adult prayer is more to do with being open to the presence of God. Words and liturgies are only a part of prayer in these adult terms. Sometimes it is through music that we can open ourselves to the presence of God, sometimes it is through art or natural beauty. So why not through tongues ... through sounds beyond words?

Those who resist this idea might think about hymns for a moment. For most church people hymns are an obvious form of worship. There is nothing strange to them about singing hymns. They are a long tried and established means of praising God.

But hymns are strange, very strange. Time and again

we sing them with only passing attention to their meaning. I often quiz people about that line in Jerusalem which asks, "And did those feet in ancient times walk upon England's mountains green?". Whose feet are these? People are often puzzled by the question. Unaware of the legend that lies behind William Blake's words, in which it is Jesus himself who walks on English soil, they have noticed neither the question marks at the end of the lines (you don't sing question marks!) nor the signals that Blake sends out that he is writing in mythical terms.

I suspect that it is frequently the first line of a hymn that establishes its meaning as we sing the other verses. But a poet of quality such as William Blake or William Cowper will have none of this. Both tended to put jags into their middle verses. "Can a woman's tender care cease towards the child she bare?" asks Cowper. A conventional hymn writer would surely have given the answer "no", leaving the singer secure and comfortable. Echoing Isaiah (49:15) Cowper perversely insists, "Yes, she may forgetful be". Yet most of us fail to notice such jags whilst singing.

Singing itself is a very odd activity. We seldom sing alone and feel foolish if caught by others doing so. We sing together. Singing can stir strong feelings and it tends to cloud meanings. It is not simply an alternative way of expressing prose. Like poetry it attracts resonances which go beyond prose. Yet, unlike poetry, it is a corporate activity which binds us together. Singing is for crowds at football matches, for social gatherings, and for services. Poetry is more for private reading or quiet contemplation.

Speaking in tongues may have affinities with both poetry and hymns. Like poetry it uses word sounds, but typically without meanings. Like hymns it is a corporate way of praising God which is centred more on feelings than thoughts.

People have different gifts which they can bring in Christ to worship. Not all will appreciate speaking in tongues. Yet from my experience with the Jesuits I came to realize that this need not be some attempt to invoke magic or replace worship with hysteria. It can properly be seen as one amongst many ways of opening ourselves to the presence of God. That indeed is adult prayer.

MEDITATION

1 Corinthians 12

29

Gifts of Healing

Gifts of the Spirit take many forms. I believe that it is a mistake to imagine that they should be restricted to the more exotic signs and wonders. Gifts of intelligence, gifts of music, gifts of friendship, can all be seen in Christ as gifts of love and thus as "gifts of the Spirit". Once churches become alive to "gifts" and resourceful about using them in the service of Christ, then we can set gifts into a much richer context.

There is an obvious trap here. As British churches continue to decline, as they have done during the course of the twentieth century, so they may be tempted to use signs and wonders to "prove" to a sceptical world that the Christian faith is "true". Great acts of healing become instant demonstrations of the truthfulness of the Gospel.

Some years ago I remember witnessing an attempt to do this. A famous "painter preacher", as he was billed, came to the town, holding rallies in the corporation hall. He preached and he painted at the same time . . . which was itself rather unusual. But then he came to the proof stage of the rally. He announced that he was going to demonstrate once and for all to the sceptics present that the Gospel is true. He was going to perform a miracle as proof.

The atmosphere in the hall sizzled. Eager people came forward for healing. Amongst them a teenage girl was brought in a wheelchair. When he spotted her coming the painter preacher stopped the music and directed that all attention should be given to her. Then laying his hands on her head, he shouted to God to heal her, finally commanding the girl to stand up. When she did the whole audience buzzed with excitement.

I was dumbfounded. The girl walked back to her seat shrieking praises to God and to the painter preacher. He in turn loudly proclaimed to the audience that this was the proof that they were looking for. The audience shouted back with cries of "Amen" and "Hallelujah".

Then I began to think of the picture of Jesus in the first three gospels. Jesus quietly touching the sick, restoring them to wholeness, and warning them to give thanks to God and to tell no one what had happened. Jesus being tempted to use miraculous powers, to turn stones into bread or to perform a wonder work by throwing himself from a pinnacle of the temple. Jesus teaching patiently through everyday stories a message about the Kingdom of God, stories laced with humour and comic events. Not much of a wonder worker here!

I thought also of the teenage girl. Was her healing sustained? Or did her muscles return to spasm soon afterwards? What if she hadn't been "healed" after that great silence? And why had the painter preacher singled out her? Did he know something that we didn't know? Was she a "plant", an innocent dupe, or a less innocent accomplice? Was he solving problems or creating them? Some experts fear that unregulated healings and exorcisms foster "devils" amongst the vulnerable where no devils existed before.

To ask all these questions is not to deny healing or to deny the gifts of the Spirit. It is simply to say that for anyone who becomes a Christian it is not necessary to become gullible. You do not have to escape from the twentieth century. The "gifts" of modern doctors and nurses are gifts in Christ. You can still use the brains that God has given you.

The Jesuits manifestly have brains and never switched them off when they opened themselves to the gifts of the Spirit. The painter preacher simply treated us as children, performing a wonder work to validate his ministry.

Gifts of the Spirit do not by-pass our brains.

MEDITATION

Mark 1:40-25

30

Redeeming Gifts

But how does all of this affect "gifts" in the everyday world? Jesus may seem so remote and the stories from the gospels, whilst they might be interesting, depict the life of a bygone age. What is the connection with ourselves?

There are two important ways of answering this question. The first returns to the idea that the world is God-given. "Gifts" in the everyday world seem to prompt us to ask about a "Giver". We can of course dismiss these promptings and maintain that the whole language of "gifts" is just a metaphor – inherited from a once religious past.

However, if we do not take that step, but keep pressing further, an obvious question arises. "If gifts can be gifts of poison as well as gifts of love, then may the Giver too be evil?" Pictures of a vengeful and spiteful God that some people have presented do seem to me to be evil. In contrast the image of God presented in Jesus is a God who cares for us and loves us sufficiently to enter our sufferings. Christ as God-given changes how we think of what really is God-given.

The second way is concerned with belonging and not just with thinking. Being a Christian is not simply about seeing God focused in Christ. It is also about belonging to a Christian community . . . about sharing the life of Christ with others. Indeed, it is in the context of Christian communities that we can learn from each other what Christian living is all about.

For me that is the importance of worship. It is not to be confused simply with prayer. Worship is something we do together. In Christian worship we pray, we sing, we listen to the Bible, we preach, we confess, and we affirm. In each of these ways we seek to grow together in Christ.

Above all, in the Eucharist we continue to share in the bread and wine. The everyday gifts of food and drink "taken" and "given" by Jesus in the gospels, continue to be "taken" and "given" by Christians all over the world.

Gifts binding us together in Christ.

MEDITATION

Romans 12:1-8

Week 6

CHRISTIAN GIVING

31

Responding to Gifts

One of the greatest joys of having small children is watching them respond to gifts. Choosing presents can be fun. On the other hand it can also be more than a bit trying – *that* might be the wrong present; or perhaps this one might be better? But best of all is to watch small children responding to what is finally bought.

The first birthday is mostly pretence, with parents giving presents and then peeping to see whether the small child is really showing pleasure. There is an absence of anticipation – no eager children waiting for the great day to arrive, hoping that they will get the very thing they have set their heart on, and inviting endless small friends to their parties. Perhaps the second too. But the third and following birthdays are for real. Small faces beaming with excitement. Presents not just given but excitedly received.

Gifts can help children to imagine. The sheer abandon of pretending to be a cowboy, or a fairy, or a lion – the small child is transported to some world of make-believe. No longer a resident of 201 Hethrop Road, she becomes an explorer in a secret African forest teeming with wild animals. Or he becomes a spaceman, daring to go where no one from 201 Hethrop Road has ever dared to go before. Dressing up can be unbelievably exciting at the age of five.

Late at night after hectic birthday parties I was always conscious of the plastic crunch. Walking on tiptoe in a child's darkened bedroom I would check that all was well.

The laughter and tears of the day had disappeared, replaced by tiny snores and sighs. Little people finally at peace. The fantasies of dreams had replaced the fantasies of games.

Then there would be a loud crunch. One of the many plastic toys would bite the carpet. And then another. Now, of course, in our day we didn't have . . . but today they have just about . . . There are plastic toys in cereal packets. There are plastic toys in crackers. Plastic soldiers, plastic computer games, plastic dolls . . . plastic everywhere. And particularly all over the floor after a small child's birthday party.

I loved running those birthday parties. Small children, for all the hard work they bring their parents, have such wondrous imaginations. The world never seems quite as thrilling again. Gifts for the very young have magical qualities which are slowly lost as we grow older.

To enhance the magic parents often invent stories about tooth fairies and Father Christmas. They collude with childhood myths. In part they may do this because they wish briefly to relive those myths themselves. Then gradually the children begin to spot contradictions. "If Father Christmas gave us all of these presents, why do we have to write thank-you letters to Aunt Ethel and to Uncle Tommy?"

They start to speculate about chimneys that are clearly blocked and about the logistics of simultaneously delivering presents to millions of children. And part of the magic is lost. For a while, if they have younger sisters or brothers, they may join their parents' collusions. They pretend to believe. But eventually such childish things are discarded . . . until one day they have children themselves.

Parents with severely handicapped children can experience deep pangs of longing as they watch other parents with their "normal" children. If only their child too could respond to gifts . . . if only they could find a present which would *make* their child respond. It isn't simply the burden of handicap which they find difficult, although that can be difficult enough. It is the seeming lack of response, the inability to express excitement, the failures to communicate.

Frances Young has written very movingly about her own experience of bringing up a severely handicapped son. Frances is a remarkable woman. She has taught at Birmingham University for over twenty years and is now Professor of Theology there. She has written several important scholarly books and she is in addition an active Methodist minister. And yet throughout her time at Birmingham she has also been mother to Arthur. Brain damaged from birth he has few words, has a minimal IQ, moves with difficulty, and remains incontinent.

Writing from her deepest experiences, and at times with painful honesty, she admits that for some years she felt that however loving she was Arthur could never respond. Her love seemed rejected. He would avoid physical contact or expressions of affection. To make matters worse, she found accepting help from others extremely distressing:

It is . . . very difficult to learn to ask for help, or even accept help generously offered. Either requires an admission that you are not self-reliant and omni-competent, and it is too humiliating. You respond with conventional polite clichés, and keep well-meaning people at arm's length. My experience makes me acutely aware of how hard it is to be on the receiving end. We all imagine that helping people is the demanding thing; but it is far more demanding to receive help with genuine grace and gratitude (*Face to Face*, T. & T. Clark, 1990, p. 41).

Giving when there is little response from the one who receives can be a lonely business.

MEDITATION

Isaiah 58.1-8

32

Being Grateful for Gifts

If gifts really are gifts of love, and are seen as gifts of love by those of us who receive them, then our most obvious response should be gratitude. Quite simply ... "Thank you".

Part of growing-up is learning to express gratitude. If the earliest stage in receiving gifts is simply learning to respond to the gifts – that is, to see them as gifts – the next is learning to express gratitude. With encouragement the mechanical thank-you letters can become more genuine expressions of gratitude. So, if we start life by becoming slowly aware of self, we become moral agents by responding to the needs of other selves.

It was Augustine who pointed out that Jesus' great command to love has three parts to it not two. Commonly we hear just two: a command to love God and a command to love our neighbours. In Mark's gospel Jesus was asked, "Which is the first of all the commandments?" He responded:

> The first is, "Hear, O Israel: the Lord our God is the one Lord, and you must love the Lord your God with all your heart, with all your soul, with all your mind, and with all your strength." The second is this: "You must love your neighbour as yourself" (Mark 12:29-31).

Augustine argued that those last two words are important. There are three loves not two: love of God, love of others, and love of self. For most of us love of self comes only too easily. Our problem is loving everyone else and loving God. The developing child learns through others that self is not all. In a context of love the child can indeed learn this. In a context of worship the child can also learn to love God. But without a context of love the child may not even love self.

Gratitude needs to be learned. I doubt if it is a "natural" response. We sometimes pretend that our pets are grateful for the things we give them. Keeping two dogs has taught me otherwise. As much as I love them I am also aware that their instant response to gifts is to snarl jealously at the other dog. Usually they act like friends. Yet they soon become enemies when gifts are at hand. If you keep two dogs you even discover the original meaning of the expression "a bone of contention".

People can behave just as badly. A recurrent theme in

the parables contained in the first three gospels is jealousy about gifts. The supposedly virtuous son in the parable of the Prodigal Son recorded by Luke is green with jealousy when his errant brother returns and is treated with such rapture by his father. The workers who have laboured all day are deeply jealous of the workers hired at the end of the day when both groups are paid equal amounts of money.

In Mark and Matthew a woman comes to Jesus with her gift of costly perfume which she proceeds to pour over his head. Those surrounding Jesus immediately show signs of jealousy. Indignantly they start muttering to each other:

"Why this waste? The perfume might have been sold for more than three hundred denarii and the money given to the poor" (Mark 14:5).

Then they begin to scold the woman. On face value they were obviously right. The costly perfume might have been sold and the money used for some other purpose. And what more worthy purpose could there have been than giving to the poor?

Luke, much earlier in his gospel, has a similar story of a woman anointing Jesus. However, in this story we are told that the woman "was living an immoral life in the town". The tut-tutting that greets her response to Jesus focuses not on the waste of expensive perfume but on her reputation. Doesn't this "prophet" know who this woman is and how bad her character is? The onlookers seem scandalized both by her behaviour and by Jesus' naïvety in allowing her to touch him.

Jesus in contrast expressed simply praise and gratitude in both stories. In Luke, addressing Simon he says:

You see this woman? I came to your house: you provided no water for my feet; but this woman has made my feet wet with her tears and wiped them with her hair. You gave me no kiss; but she has been kissing my feet ever since I came in. You did not anoint my head with oil; but she has anointed my feet with myrrh. So, I tell you, her great love proves that her many sins have been forgiven (Luke 7:44-47).

A few verses later in their gospels, both Mark and Matthew after giving us their version of the story recount how Jesus took bread and wine, gave thanks to God, and gave them to his disciples. The links between "gifts", gratitude, and finally worship, are clear. Worship is first and foremost our expression of gratitude for all that God has given.

I have argued that seeing Christ as God-given, and sharing the gifts of bread and wine in Christ, change our understanding of "gifts". In the everyday world "gifts" can be creative or poisonous. They are exciting, but they can also be destructive. In Christ "gifts" take on new depth. We are given a new vision of God as Giver. God's "gifts" in Christ are gifts of real love.

What should our response be to *these* gifts?

MEDITATION

Matthew 20:1-15

33

Using Gifts

If gratitude is our first truly adult response to gifts, then their responsible use should be our second. If we have gifts, we should use them. If something really is a "gift" then personal conceit or boasting are inappropriate. It is quite tempting for those with high profile "gifts" – in art, music, maths, sport, or whatever – to be conceited. The extreme adulation that surrounds high achievers in the arts or in sport doubtless fosters conceit. All those curtain calls at the end of an opera, the groupies who pursue pop-stars, or the kissing and laps of honour that have crept into sport. It is not difficult to see how the "gifted" become conceited.

Yet natural abilities, or God-given abilities, are not in themselves anything to boast about. Quite the opposite. Once we identify "gifts" as "gifts of God", our concern should be rather to use those gifts to God's glory, not to our own.

However, even here there is a danger. Gifts can appear to be too exotic. By focusing on special "gifts" – in art, music, chess or sport – the rest of us can appear ungifted. "Gifts" appear to be for the few, not for the many. Even "gifts of the Spirit" have sometimes, and quite falsely, been seen as the privilege of the few. So a few have "gifts" of healing or speaking in tongues, whereas most of us are ungifted . . .

Nothing could be further from Paul's vision of "gifts of the Spirit". He repeatedly insisted that all have gifts. These will undoubtedly differ, some people having one gift and others having another. Yet in the Christian community – what he termed the Body of Christ – all gifts of the Spirit should contribute to a single goal:

> There are varieties of gifts, but the same Spirit. There are varieties of service, but the same Lord. There are varieties of activity, but in all of them and in everyone the same God is active. In each of us the Spirit is seen to be at work for some useful purpose (1 Corinthians 12:4-7).

Not in a few, but in each of us. So, Paul's logic insists, each of us must use our "gifts". They are given to us in Christ to be used, not to be wasted.

Together these gifts contribute to a single, living Christian community. Paul seemed ever conscious that Christians are not just individuals. They are part of a larger fellowship. The modern saying that "I can be a perfectly good Christian without going to church" would have been very alien to him. For Paul, being a Christian entailed being an active part of the Christian community. Christianity was not just about thinking or acting privately. It involved being a part of a worshipping community.

This corporate dimension to gifts is also evident in this famous chapter on gifts of the Spirit in 1 Corinthians:

> But all these gifts are the activity of one and the same Spirit, distributing them to each individual at will. Christ is like a single body with its many limbs and organs, which, many as they are, together make up one body; for in the one Spirit we were all brought into one body by baptism, whether Jews or Greeks, slaves or

free; we were all given that one Spirit to drink. A body is not a single organ, but many (1 Corinthians 12:11-14).

Gifts of all types can be seen as gifts of the Spirit precisely when they are used in Christ. Whether we use our gifts directly in the service of churches, or whether we use them in the wider world as an expression of our commitment to Christ, they are truly gifts of the Spirit. Whatever gifts we each have, and however modest we may feel them to be, they *are* gifts of the Spirit.

MEDITATION

1 Peter 4:7-11

34

Giving Time

Prison is sometimes described as "doing time" or "serving time". A loss of time is deemed to cancel a debt to society, or perhaps just time is forfeited by society. Time is lost. Time given, in contrast, is time used for others.

Already in the short history of AIDS some remarkable stories of "giving time" are emerging. Some with AIDS determine to live out their few remaining months or years for others with AIDS. Some with AIDS reject entirely the label "AIDS sufferers" and talk positively instead of "the gift of AIDS". Dying children helping grieving parents, dying friends comfort and care for each other.

Because AIDS hits young people who would normally expect to live for decades, it highlights something that we must all eventually face. We will all die. Our time is finite and limited. It can be given for others or spent mainly on ourselves. For all of us time is a "gift". AIDS serves to focus attention on something that is open to all of us.

Whenever I visit the elderly I am impressed at the gift of patience that many who care for them have. Working continuously with the sharp minds of university students it is all too easy to become impatient of the small-talk which passes the day for many people. It also becomes quite difficult to concentrate on stories told and re-told by the very old. In contrast those caring for the elderly often have boundless patience. They can listen and listen again and still express surprise and astonishment at stories they already know by heart.

Such patience is surely a gift, and an immensely valuable one. I doubt if many who show patience in this way think of this as a gift. Too often I hear them saying, "I am just a care assistant. I didn't get any O Levels or GCEs. I don't have the brains of all those clever doctors and nurses." Or again, "I am only a home help. I don't have any gifts. Anybody could do what I do."

The reality is frequently quite different. They have patience well beyond the scope of many of those they regard as "gifted". They show daily acts of care which should be the envy of others. And in the day to day life of the elderly or the handicapped it is their presence and friendship which endures. Such care, patience and friendship are indeed real gifts.

Frances Young again writes movingly from her own experience. She recounts how she slowly came to terms with visiting the handicapped:

A few years ago I still found the presence of handicapped people *en masse* profoundly distressing. At times I even had to pluck up courage to go to events at my own son's school. But I had reached the point when I felt I had worked through all the hang-ups and perhaps had something to give. I found again that I was receiving more than I gave. To be obliged to switch off from all the rush of teaching and doing things once a week, and just to go and be with people for whom life was basic and simple, for some of whom verbal communication was difficult or impossible, became profoundly important ... A little old lady, deaf and speechless, played peep-bo with a cuddly scarf, and the two of us were close in our smiles and embraces of affection ... Then there was Dennis ... Dennis had no speech and seemed to sit all day with a rather glum look on his face, playing with his fingers. I suggested we might go out, and immediately he got up, clearly understanding language even if he had none ... And on each occasion at some point on our walk, his set face would break into a heavenly smile (*Face to Face*, pp. 101-2).

Giving time to the elderly, to the handicapped, to the desperate, to those in prison, is something that all can do – young or old. In a busy world it is easy to be so preoccupied with our own roles and problems that we fail to stop and look to the needs of others around us. We become globules of activity, keeping our immediate families to ourselves, whilst ignoring the old folk's home or the prison down the road. Of course we also try to put off the awful thought that one day we too may be old or that we too might be amongst the needy. We too may be lonely. We too may wish that others could stop their business for a moment and give us some of their time.

The parable of the Sheep and the Goats, recounted near the end of Matthew's gospel, has for long been one of my favourites. It is set in a chapter which insists through three different parables that we should use our gifts because the Kingdom of God is near. The first parable is that of ten girls waiting for a bridegroom. Five wisely think ahead and bring extra fuel for their lamps, but five do not. The second parable, that of the Talents, tells of a man going abroad who entrusts his servants with differing amounts of money. Two use their money (talents) to make more money, but the third simply buries it.

The third parable is that of the Sheep and the Goats. This great parable has inspired much Christian service over the centuries. Its focus is not upon exotic gifts but upon the everyday gifts of kindness and care. In the parable the king blesses one group with these words:

> You have my Father's blessing; come, take possession of the kingdom that has been ready for you since the world was made. For when I was hungry, you gave me food; when thirsty, you gave me drink; when I was a stranger, you took me into your home; when naked, you clothed me; when I was ill, you came to my help; when in prison, you visited me (Matthew 25:34-36).

The group is astonished to be blessed in this way and asks

when was it that they did all these things to the King. Their question, as so often in the parables, is made particularly ironic by being addressed to the King. Surely he has not been in prison or hungry or in need of any material kind?

The king's reply goes to the very heart of Christian living:

"Truly I tell you: anything you did for one of my brothers here, however insignificant, you did for me."

MEDITATION
Job 31

35

Giving Money

Once I thought that the giving of money was easy. What was difficult was deciding the amount. There was never a shortage of deserving causes. Then I met a major philanthropist, someone who had literally given millions of pounds away in his lifetime. I had little concept before I came to know William Leech of just how difficult and demanding true Christian giving really is.

Perhaps I should explain that the chair of applied theology that I hold at Newcastle University was made possible in the first place by his extraordinary generosity. For a period of nearly forty years he was responsible for over sixty million pounds being given to five major church charities. Five years ago these charities were approached by representatives of the religious studies department at Newcastle University to endow a research chair there in honour of William Leech and to further the work of churches engaged in outreach.

As a result of being appointed to the chair I came to know William Leech myself. He invited me to his house to talk about my work, to drink some of his malt whisky, and to admire his spectacular greenhouse. His passion for the Christian faith, for whisky and for plants was just about equally divided. He was an enthusiast for life at many levels. And as we became friends so he began to consult me on church issues.

One afternoon he asked me and two others to go with him to a presentation from a Christian group seeking extensive funding. It was soon clear that the project was imaginative but unrealistic. William Leech, although almost ninety at the time, listened patiently for two hours. At the end he gently probed the economic arrangements the group had in mind.

When I went to see him some days later I asked whether he had decided to fund the project. Only then did I discover that this was just one of eighty other requests that he was currently considering, a quarter of which would receive some funding. Despite a whole afternoon spent listening to the group and a deep enthusiasm for their faith, he had decided that their financial arrangements were insufficiently strict.

Over the next few months he regularly talked about the various projects he was considering funding through his

Trust. Always it was the same. Deep care and faith combined with a sharp business eye for sloppy financial arrangements. He was unfailingly concerned that the disadvantaged should be given the highest priority — especially in the Third World. He constantly encouraged other wealthy friends to give generously and responsibly. And he always gave because he believed that God had first given to him.

When I made my final visit to him, three days before he died, I asked him for the first time whether he would like me to pray with him. I will long treasure his response: "There is nothing that would give me greater pleasure."

Casual giving is easy. Tossing coins to beggars or putting small change into collecting boxes on flag days is easy. Sacrificial giving is not. Luke alone, again with his sharp eye for the dangers of wealth, recounts the story of the widow's mites:

> As Jesus looked up and saw rich people dropping their gifts into the chest of the temple treasury, he noticed a poor widow putting in two tiny coins. "I tell you this," he said: "this poor widow has given more than any of them; for those others who have given had more than enough, but she, with less than enough, has given all she had to live on" (Luke 21:1-4).

Giving away millions of pounds responsibly is not easy either. Ten pence even to the most alcoholic beggar will probably not make that much difference (although food would surely be better). But a million pounds to the wrong cause could mean disaster. By giving irresponsibly we can actually make things considerably worse . . . as charities like Christian Aid or Oxfam know only too well.

That we should all give, and give generously, seems to be required by our Christian faith. But that we should give responsibly and only after careful thought and prayer seems also to be required.

MEDITATION

Acts 20:32-35

36

Giving Love

Throughout this book I have struggled with the idea that gifts can be poisonous as well as loving. Gifts intended in love can turn instead to poison. And gifts once used poisonously can in Christ be transformed into gifts of love.

Of all the gifts in Christ it is love which is by far the most important. Giving love stands at the very heart of Christian living.

Repeatedly in the gospels Jesus reminds his followers about the gift of love. In Matthew's gospel love is at the centre of the great Sermon on the Mount that he presents:

You have heard that they were told, "Love your neighbour and hate your enemy." But what I tell you is this: Love your enemies and pray for your persecutors; only so can you be children of your heavenly Father, who causes the sun to rise on good and bad alike, and sends the rain on the innocent and the wicked. If you love only those who love you, what reward can you expect? Even the tax-collectors do as much as that (Matthew 5:43-47).

In his letters Paul became most lyrical when he was writing about love. For me the two finest passages in his letters are about the gift of love in Christ.

The first of these passages is in the Letter to the Romans. At about the mid-point of this letter there is a magnificent crescendo. It has clearly been written by one who has known pain, ridicule and suffering. And perhaps too he has known the acute wrenches of doubt that converts typically feel at moments of crisis. Yet through all of this Paul wrote:

Then what can separate us from the love of Christ? Can affliction or hardship? Can persecution, hunger, nakedness, danger, or sword? "We are being done to death for your sake all day long," as scripture says; "we have been treated like sheep for slaughter" – and yet, throughout it all, overwhelming victory is ours through him who loved us. For I am convinced that there is nothing in death or life, in the realm of spirits or super-human powers, in the world as it is or the world as it shall be, in the forces of the universe, in heights or depths – nothing in all creation that can separate us from the love of God in Christ Jesus our Lord (Romans 8:35-39).

The second passage is even more poignant. Paul's description of "gifts of the Spirit" in 1 Corinthians is followed in the next chapter by his superb depiction of love. I must confess that sometimes Paul's arguments make me quite angry. Judged from a perspective of the modern world he sometimes appears belligerent and overbearing. His understanding of women and marriage seem to be especially restricted. Yet for his depiction of love I can excuse him almost anything.

> I may speak in tongues of men or of angels, but if I have no love, I am a sounding gong or a clanging cymbal. I may have the gift of prophecy and the knowledge of every hidden truth; I may have faith enough to move mountains; but if I have no love, I am nothing (1 Corinthians 13:1-2).

Without love all is empty. Even giving, and giving on a heroic scale, without love is empty:

> I may give all I possess to the needy, I may give my body to be burnt, but if I have no love, I gain nothing by it (1 Corinthians 13:3).

At the end of an examination of "gifts" these are remarkable words. Giving without love is empty.

And love is a "gift" that all can give. Love does not require special "gifts" of music, art, maths, sport, or whatever. Love does not demand particular types of intelligence. Indeed, all of these gifts can at times stand in the way of love. Love does not require fine words. Lovers can sometimes be rendered almost speechless. Rather:

> Love is patient and kind. Love envies no one, is never boastful, never conceited, never rude; love is never selfish, never quick to take offence. Love keeps no score

of wrongs, takes no pleasure in the sins of others, but delights in the truth. There is nothing love cannot face; there is no limit to its faith, its hope, its endurance. Love will never come to an end (1 Corinthians 13:4-8).

It is love which is the greatest "gift" . . . God's love for us and our response in love to ourselves, to each other, and to God.

MEDITATION

1 Corinthians 15:53–58